COLOR OF RIPE FRUIT

WILD
BERRIES & FRUITS
FIELD GUIDE <u>ILLINOIS, IOWA AND MISSOURI</u>

by Teresa Marrone

Adventure Publications
Cambridge, Minnesota

ACKNOWLEDGMENTS

Special thanks to Mike Krebill for his guiding, assistance, hospitality, friendship and sharing of knowledge; to Lisa Schindler, for her help with the maypops; and to Bruce Bohnenstingl, the world's best photo assistant and berry scout.

Thanks to Mike Krebill for his review of the book.

Cover and book design by Jonathan Norberg

Flower anatomy illustration by Julie Martinez

Edited by Brett Ortler

Photo credits by photographer and page number:
Cover photos: Black raspberry, blueberry, buttonbush and rose hips by Teresa Marrone

All photos by Teresa Marrone unless noted.
Steven J. Baskauf: 125 (both), 309 **Ted Bodner/Southern Weed Science Society, Bugwood.org:** 273 **Jim Conrad:** 213 (inset) **Will Cook:** 253, 289 (both), 297 (main) **Shirley Denton:** 301 (inset) **Derek E. Goertz:** 231 (bottom half page) **jaHar.pix:** 255 (inset) **Sonnia Hill:** 277 (inset) **Stu Kogge:** 231 (bottom inset) **Mike Krebill:** 89 (fruit inset), 257 **Uli Lorimer:** 115 **Rachel E. Lyons:** 85 (main) **Ernie Marx:** 45 **Maslowski Wildlife Productions:** 163 **Lorena Babcock Moore:** 73, 225 **Walter Muma:** 275, 317 (both) **J. S. Peterson:** 207 **Don Poggensee:** 97 **Bron Praslicka:** 213 (main) **Lisa Kelley Schindler:** 51 (main) **Per Verdonk:** 81 (split capsule inset) **Ryann Waite:** 67 (inset) **www.sunfarm.com:** 101

10 9 8 7 6 5 4 3 2

Wild Berries & Fruits Field Guide of Illinois, Iowa and Missouri
Copyright © 2010 by Teresa Marrone
Published by Adventure Publications
An imprint of AdventureKEEN
310 Garfield Street South
Cambridge, Minnesota 55008
(800) 678-7006
www.adventurepublications.net
Printed in China
ISBN 978-1-59193-248-2 (pbk.)

TABLE OF CONTENTS

Introduction

The Berries and Fruits

Helpful Resources and Bibliography

ABOUT THIS BOOK

Numerous field guides are available to aid in flower identification, but few address the fruiting stage of the plant. Those that do usually add a footnote or a small photo of the fruit. But the fruiting stage is critical to the plant and interesting to observers of nature as well. This book is specifically about that glorious stage in a plant's life when it fulfills its purpose by producing fruits to help it reproduce.

This book is unique as it was written with the forager in mind, and especially for foragers interested in taking home their finds and using them in recipes and in the kitchen. For this reason, this book makes references to *Cooking with Wild Berries & Fruits of Illinois, Iowa and Missouri*, a companion cookbook which includes recipes, handy tips, and different uses for many of the edible species found in this book.

In addition to showing edible berries and fruits, this book also identifies those berries and fruits which are inedible—even toxic. This information is critical to anyone who is faced with an unknown plant and wishes to know if its fruit is edible. It's also just plain interesting to see all the fascinating and, often, lovely fruits produced by plants, whether that fruit is edible or not.

Photos in this book focus primarily on the fruits, in all their up-close-and -personal glory. However, plant structure and leaf form are also critical to proper identification. The photos here attempt to show the key identification points of each plant; this information is also covered in the text that accompanies each photo. Features that are key to distinguishing a plant from one with similar appearance are in green type in the text; study these points with particular care when looking at a plant.

Habitat and season are also important when attempting to identify a plant. Both of these are covered in the text. Range maps for each species show approximate locations in Illinois, Iowa, and Missouri where each plant is likely to be found. Helpful information that allows the reader to compare similar plants provides additional insight that will aid in positive identification. Finally, each plant account includes short notes, which may feature interesting tidbits about the plant, how it has been used for food or medicine, or information on how the plant is used by birds and other wildlife.

Common names of plants are often confusing. People in different areas use different names for the same plant, and, sometimes, the same common name is used for two—or more—very different plants. All plant accounts in this book include the common name usually used by the United States Department of Agriculture, and occasionally another common name. More importantly, the scientific name is listed for each species; this is the most definitive nomenclature of all.

THE RANGE MAPS

The maps showing plant ranges are based on information from the United States Department of Agriculture, the United States Geological Survey, and the United States Forest Service (see pg. 318 for website addresses); much of the Iowa range information came from *The Vascular Plants of Iowa*, and some of the Missouri range data came from *Shrubs and Woody Vines of Missouri* (see Helpful Resources and Bibliography on pg. 318 for publication information). These sources have been supplemented with state-specific surveys from natural-resources agencies, universities and herbariums, as well as the author's personal knowledge and experience.

Range maps are a useful tool, but are not an absolute authority. Plants rarely follow state or county lines, but most plant surveyors do when reporting their data to the USDA or other authorities. Further, some counties have not submitted data or been surveyed, and so do not appear on the lists used by government agencies. The maps in this book are approximations, and it is possible to find a plant in an area not shown on the range map (or, conversely, to be unable to find a plant in an area indicated on the map). In some cases, county-specific data is not available, yet the plant is known to grow in the state. In such cases, the state is colored with a lighter shade of the color used in that section; this indicates that the plant is present in the state, but does not show specific areas where it may be found.

WHAT IS A FRUIT?

Since this book is all about fruit, it's worth discussing exactly what that term means in the context of the book. At its most basic, a fruit is the ripened part of a plant that disperses seeds; this includes things like pea pods, wheat heads and nuts. In everyday usage, however, most of us consider only fleshy, juicy, seed-bearing structures, such as blueberries, watermelon and apples, to be "fruit." The short and fairly non-scientific discussion that follows will provide helpful reference for the discussion of various fruit types discussed later.

Like most living things, plants have male and female parts. Depending on species, they may exist together in one flower as illustrated below, or may grow in distinct male or female flowers. (Sometimes the male and female parts don't look anything like this, as with pine trees; then again, these plants don't produce what we think of as fruit.) The female part of the plant, at the center of the flower, is collectively called the *pistil*. It consists of an ovary, topped with a long style, capped with the stigma. The ovary is a case containing one or more carpels, which are ovule-bearing structures containing one or more ovules, or eggs; typically, several carpels are fused together within the ovary, but in a few cases the carpel is single.

The male part of the plant is collectively called the *stamen*. It consists of the pollen-bearing element called the anther, which is supported by the filament, a thin structure that raises the anther above the base of the flower. (The flower petals are there to attract pollinators, by the way—the plant world's version of the little black dress.)

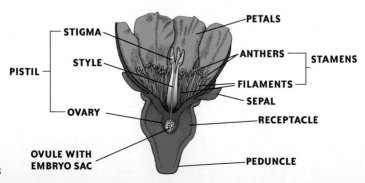

8

Seeds develop when pollen is introduced into ripe eggs. This service is performed by insects, animals or the wind; regardless of the method, the pollen is deposited onto the sticky stigma, where it germinates, sending the male nuclei down the style to fertilize the eggs. The ovary swells as the seeds mature. The result of all this activity is the fruit—a fleshy structure carrying the fertilized seeds.

Within that narrow definition, there are several types of fruit. Here are short, simple definitions of the types of fruits that are included in this book; please also look at page 19 to see what is *not* included.

BERRIES

A berry is a simple fleshy fruit containing one or more carpels (ovule bearing structures), each with one or more seeds. The seed coating, or endocarp, is relatively soft. Examples include grapes (pg. 196), gooseberries (pgs. 54, 136, 202 and 264), currants (pgs. 134, 266) and blueberries (pg. 226).

Grapes

Gooseberries

Currants

Blueberries

DRUPES

A drupe, sometimes called a stone fruit, is a simple fleshy fruit with a seed (or on occasion, seeds) contained in a hard pit, or stone. The hard outside of the pit is the endocarp (seed coating). Examples include plums (pgs. 180, 182, 212), autumn olives (pg. 160) and choke-cherries (pg. 154).

American wild plum

Autumn olive

Common chokecherry

COMPOUND DRUPES

A compound drupe is a fleshy fruit formed from a single flower, but composed of many drupes, each containing one seed. Compound drupes are typically thought of as "seedy" because they contain so many seeds, each with its own endocarp (seed coating). Examples include red raspberries (pg. 130) and common blackberries (pg. 270).

Red raspberry

Common blackberry

Mulberry

MULTIPLE FRUIT

An unusual fruit structure in which a single fruit is formed from multiple flowers that grow closely together in a cluster. Multiple fruits in this book are Osage orange (pg. 60) and mulberries (pg. 172). Figs and pineapples are multiple fruits that don't grow in our region.

POMES

A pome is a pseudocarp, a simple fruit with flesh developed from the receptacle (the end of the flower stalk) rather than the ovary. In pomes, the receptacle surrounds the ovary, and seeds are contained in the carpel, which becomes papery. Examples in this book include crabapples (pg. 174), hawthorns (pg. 186), mountain ash (pg. 86) and serviceberries (pg. 208).

Crabapple

Hawthorn

Mountain ash

Serviceberry

OTHER TYPES OF FRUIT

Strawberry

Pseudocarps are fruits whose flesh develops from a part other than the ovary. Pomes (pg. 11) are one type. Another is the strawberry (pg. 92); unlike a pome, however, the strawberry carries its seeds on the surface rather than in the center of the fruit.

Wild cucumber

Pepos are berry-like fruits with a very tough rind developed from the receptacle (in most fruits, the skin is developed from the ovary). Wild cucumber (pg. 52) is a pepo that is in this book; others which are not in this book are melons and gourds.

Purple trillium

Capsules are dry, non-fleshy fruits that split at maturity to scatter their seeds. Most capsule fruits don't resemble anything we'd think of as fruit and are not included here; however, several, including trillium (pg. 98) have a large, fleshy capsule that looks like fruit, so they are included.

Common juniper

Cones are fruits that consist of scales (sporophylls) arranged in an overlapping or spiral fashion around a central core; seeds are developed between the scales. Common juniper (pg. 228) and eastern red cedar (pg. 238) are included in this book because their cones look berry-like.

HOW FRUITS ARE ARRANGED ON THE STEM

Fruits may grow singly on a stem, or in clusters. Locations also vary; fruits may grow at the ends of branches, along the branches, or in leaf axils. Here are a few of the common arrangements and locations.

Common chokecherry

A *raceme* is a cluster of fruit growing on a central stem; each fruit has its own stalk, and all stalks are of equal length. At left is a raceme of chokecherries. Racemes can also be branched, with each branch having a small raceme; this is called a *panicle*.

A rounded *umbrella-like cluster*, called an *umbel*, contains numerous fruit stalks that grow from a common point on the main fruiting stem. All stalks are the same length, so the cluster is rounded. The highbush cranberry shown at right is an example. Another type of umbrella-like cluster is called a *corymb*; in this arrangement, fruit stalks vary in length so that all fruits are aligned in a flat-topped cluster.

Highbush cranberry

The *leaf axil* is the point at which the leaf joins the stem; many fruits are attached at the axils. At right are glossy buckthorn fruits growing from the leaf axils.

Glossy buckthorn

Silky dogwood

Fruits also grow at the end of the stem; at left is a cluster of silky dogwood fruits growing at the end of a stem.

LEAF FORM AND ARRANGEMENT

Leaves are one of the most important features to consider when attempting to identify a plant. Their shape, the way they attach to the plant, characteristics of the edge, and, of course, size and color must all be considered. Botanists use many terms to describe these things in exacting detail; this book does not reach so far, using terms geared to the layperson. Here is a brief overview of some of these terms.

Amur honeysuckle

Form and arrangement are the first characteristics to look at. The leaves of this honeysuckle are *simple*—a single leaf blade is attached to the stem of the plant. The leaf is narrowly oval, with a rounded base and pointed tip. Looking closer, we see that the leaf has a short *petiole*—the stemlet that attaches the leaf to the stem. The leaf is attached *oppositely*—directly across the stem from another leaf. Its edge is *smooth*, not jagged or toothy. It is deep green and glossy above. The *midrib*—the long line that divides the leaf in two—is pale.

Gooseberry

Although the gooseberry leaves at left are also called simple, there's a lot more going on. They are *lobed*, meaning that each leaf, although whole and undivided, has several distinct sections, rather like a maple leaf. The petiole (stemlet) is much longer than that of the honeysuckle above. The leaves are arranged *alternately* on the stem, with some distance between the points where each leaf attaches to the stem. Leaf veins are noticeable but not prominent, and the midvein does not stand out as on the honeysuckle leaf. Leaf color is medium green above, and the surface is somewhat *rough*; leaf edges have *rounded teeth*, and the base is broad.

Black raspberry

Compound leaves look like a small stem with numerous leaves; the entire grouping is called a *blade*. Individual leaves on each blade are called *leaflets*. The blade is a true leaf, with a bud at its base; leaflets don't have buds. This black raspberry has three-part compound leaves—each blade has three leaflets, which have *sharply toothed edges*. Compound leaves can have a dozen or more leaflets on each blade. If they are arranged in a row along the blade stem, the blade is said to be pinnately compound; see mountain ash on pg. 86 for an example.

White baneberry

Some compound leaves are even more complicated, consisting of several compound leaves attached to the blade stem. The white baneberry pictured at right has *doubly compound* leaves: the blade has three compound leaves, each with five to seven leaflets. This plant has three doubly compound leaves: the one at the top, which also is bearing the fruiting stalk, and the two that are going off to the sides near the bottom of the photo.

Virginia creeper

The final type of compound leaf is called *palmately compound*. As shown by the leaves of this Virginia creeper, the leaflets all radiate from a central point, rather than growing on a blade stem.

Note that characteristics of the individual leaves shown here, other than leaf form, are not always as shown. For example, a simple leaf can have a long or short petiole (or no petiole); its edges may be pointed or smooth, and it may grow alternately.

LEAF ATTACHMENT

The previous pages showed some examples of leaf attachment; this page gives additional examples of those, as well as a few others that were not shown. Note that the text discusses the attachment of a leaf to the stem, but the same attachment styles could also apply to the attachment of a leaflet to a blade stem (on a compound leaf).

Crabapple

Many leaves are attached to the stem by a *petiole*, which can be defined as a leaf stemlet. Petioles can be long or short, smooth or hairy, round or flattened, and any color found in nature. The petioles on the crabapple leaves shown at left are long, smooth and greenish.

Some leaves are *sessile*—they attach directly to the stem. The false Solomon's seal shown below left is an example of this. *Perfoliate* leaves, like those of the large-flowered bellwort shown below right, have a base that extends slightly beyond the stem, giving the impression that the stem is growing up through the leaf.

False Solomon's seal

Large-flowered bellwort

Clasping leaves have no petiole (stemlet); the base of the leaf clasps, or slightly surrounds the stem, but does not extend beyond it. Smooth Solomon's seal, pictured at right, is an example of a clasping leaf.

Smooth Solomon's seal

Nodding trillium

Sometimes, three or more leaves grow from a common point of attachment. This style of leaf arrangement is called *whorled*, and is seen in the trillium photo at left.

To the botanist, leaf attachment and leaf arrangement are different discussions; for the layperson, the distinction is not important. The whorled example seems to cross into both categories.

LEAF SHAPES

Leaves and leaflets take numerous shapes; here are the most common. Note that leaves may taper on one or both ends, may have rounded or heart-shaped bases with pointed tips, or any number of combinations.

Lowbush blueberry

Oval leaves (sometimes called elliptic leaves) are the most familiar. At left are the oval leaves of blueberries.

Lance-shaped or sword-like leaves are long and slender; often, sides are almost parallel for much of the leaves' length. Below left are the lance-shaped leaves of starry false Solomon's seal.

Paddle-shaped leaves are narrow at the base, widening at or above the midpoint; they typically have a rounded tip. Below right are the paddle-shaped leaves of barberry.

Starry false Solomon's seal

Barberry

SAFETY AND PLANT IDENTIFICATION

If you are using this book to identify plants just for pleasure, that's great; hopefully, you will find what you're looking for and may even enjoy keeping a life list of fruits spotted. However, if you are planning to eat any of the fruits you identify, it is critical to follow good identification practices. Before sampling a plant's fruit, determine the plant's overall structure, its color, its leaf and stem arrangement, fruit appearance and characteristics. The photos and text in this book are as clear and concise as possible; however, they are not exhaustive. Sometimes, a plant looks slightly different than those photographed, and identification becomes a bit of a guessing game. It's prudent to consult more than one guidebook before consuming something you've foraged, and I strongly urge you to do so. The Helpful Resources on pgs. 318-319 will give you some sources that may be helpful. This extra effort is worth it; a mistake could cause illness or, in rare cases, death.

It's also important to note that individual reaction to foods varies; to some, the everyday peanut is a ballpark snack, while to others, it can cause life-threatening complications if ingested. Reactions to wild foods are not always well-documented or predictable; when you're eating an unfamiliar wild food, try just a small portion at first.

Also, remember that many wild foods are edible only at a certain stage of growth, or with certain special preparations. That information is beyond the scope of this book; however, the notes and information with each species account point out possible issues with the various fruits you may find. If the text has any indications that special preparations may be required, or that ripeness is critical to edibility, it is your responsibility to learn what is required to make certain your foraged fruits are edible and safe.

Some fruits are edible but not palatable; these are noted as "edible" in most cases, although in a few cases they are noted as "not edible" because they really aren't worth experimenting with. Others may cause

stomach upset or other relatively minor difficulties; these are noted as "not edible." Some, however, can kill if enough is ingested; and in a few cases, the amount is shockingly little. These plants are listed as "toxic" and contain the skull-and-crossbones symbol at left. Pay attention to this. It's not worth taking chances.

WHAT IS NOT INCLUDED IN THIS BOOK

In general, the fruits included in this book are those which most people would identify as fruits. Capsules such as those produced by poppies, maple-tree wings (samaras), and dry seeds such as sunflower seeds and wheat kernels, would not likely be considered a fruit, so are not in this book. Here are some other things which are not included.

Nuts, such as these shagbark hickories, are large, dry fruits with hard seedcoats; they usually contain a single seed. Nuts are indehiscent, meaning that they remain closed when mature

Legumes are pods, often quite narrow, that contain pea-like or bean-like seeds. Legumes are dehiscent, meaning that they dry out and split open, releasing their seeds. Pods of American vetch are pictured at left.

Follicles are dry, dehiscent fruits that dry out and split on one side to scatter their seeds. The fruit of a milkweed, a very common follicle, is pictured at left.

Galls are not a fruit, but rather a swelling in the stem of a plant caused by an insect. The round bulge on this anemone could be easily mistaken for a fruit.

NOT RIPE YET!

Most berries and fruits start out green, changing to another color when they are ripe; a few, however, remain green even when ripe. Others are a color other than green even though they are still unripe. This book is organized by the color of the ripe fruit.* If you encounter a plant that has green (or obviously unripe) fruit on it, how can you find it in this book if you don't know what color it will be when it *is* ripe? This is of particular interest if the fruit will be edible when it's ripe; you can note the location of the unripe fruit and return later in the season to harvest it.

To help, here are photos of some edible berries and fruits in the unripe stage, along with information that points you to the correct page in this book. Note that gooseberries (pgs. 54, 136, 202 and 264) are edible in both the green and the ripe stages, so they appear in more than one color section.

Lowbush blueberry (pg. 226)

Wild grape (pg. 196)

Red raspberry (pg. 130)

Common blackberry (pg. 270)

Common elderberry (pg. 204)

Thimbleberry (pg. 132)

Rose hip (pg. 140)

Guelder rose (pg. 156)

Sand cherry (pg. 262)

American wild plum (pg. 180)

* Some plants, such as glossy buckthorn (pgs. 168, 290), are encountered so frequently in the unripe stage, or ripen so slowly, that they are shown in two sections: first in the section that shows the unripe fruit, and also in the section that corresponds with the color of the ripe fruit. A few plants, such as false Solomon's seal (pg. 36) and eastern poison ivy (pg. 48), are shown in the green section because their fruits are green for most of the summer.

BE CERTAIN, BE SAFE: WILD GRAPES

Wild grapes are a prime wild edible; they're delicious and abundant. However, several other vining plants in our area have inedible or toxic fruits that appear somewhat similar to wild grapes. Fortunately, it's easy to distinguish between them if you pay attention when harvesting.

Below is a photo of riverbank grapes (pg. 196). On the next page, you'll find photos of some fruits that appear similar. Key identification points also help you distinguish between grapes and these other fruits.

Riverbank grape

Canada moonseed (pg. 198)

Heartleaf peppervine (pg, 200)

Virginia creeper (pg. 222)

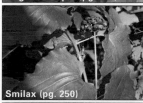

Smilax (pg. 250)

Cupseed (pg. 254)

LEAVES

Grape: Shallow to deep lobes, toothed edges

Canada moonseed: Three to seven shallow lobes, smooth edges

Peppervine: Heart-shaped, toothed edges

Virginia creeper: Palmately compound, coarsely toothed edges

Smilax: Heart-shaped or oval, typically smooth edges

Cupseed: Palmately lobed or heart-shaped, typically smooth edges

TENDRILS

Grape: Coiling tendrils

Canada moonseed: No tendrils

Peppervine: Branched tendrils

Virginia creeper: Sucker-foot tendrils

Smilax: Varies with species

Cupseed: No tendrils

FRUITS

Grape: Purplish/blackish with a bloom; large, long cluster on sturdy stalk; one to six seeds per fruit (delicious)

Canada moonseed: Purplish with a bloom; loose clusters on thin stalk; single flat, crescent-shaped seed (toxic)

Peppervine: Multi-colored, speckled; wide, loose clusters (inedible)

Virginia creeper: Bluish-purple with a bloom; loose clusters on hot-pink stemlets (inedible)

Smilax: Bluish-black with a bloom; rounded cluster on stiff stalk (edible)

Cupseed: Black, no bloom; long, tight cluster (inedible)

RIPENING CALENDAR FOR EDIBLE FRUIT

	May	June
Gooseberry (pg. 54, 136, 202, 264)		* * *
Ground-plum milkvetch (pg. 96)		
Strawberry (pg. 92)		
Serviceberry (pg. 208)		
Black raspberry (pg. 258)		
Red, white mulberry (pg. 172)		
Blueberry (pg. 226)		
Dewberry (pg. 118, 260, 272)		
Black huckleberry (pg. 268)		
Currant (pg. 134, 266)		
Red raspberry (pg. 130)		
Crabapple (pg. 174)		
Fragrant sumac (pg. 128)		
Mahaleb cherry (pg. 176)		
Mock strawberry (pg. 110)		
Goji berry (pg. 138)		
Common blackberry (pg. 270)		
Thimbleberry, purple-flowering raspberry (pg. 132)		
Mayapple (pg. 64)		
Black cherry (pg. 296)		
Peach (pg. 84)		
Sand cherry (pg. 262)		
Bunchberry (pg. 102)		
Pin cherry (pg. 178)		
Common elderberry (pg. 204)		
Wild plum (pg. 180, 182, 212)		
Yellow passionflower (pg. 224)		
Farkleberry, deerberry (pg. 288)		

* edible when green in color

Timing may vary by several weeks from the southern to the northern part of our area, and also may vary from year to year depending on weather. Date ranges shown here are an average; fruits in any given area may ripen a week or two earlier—or later—than shown.

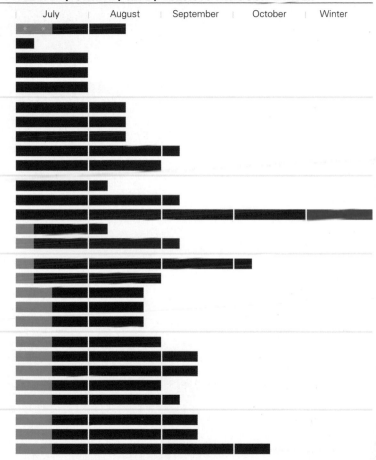

RIPENING CALENDAR FOR EDIBLE FRUIT (CONTINUED)

	May	June
Wild grape (pg. 196)		
Winged sumac (pg. 210)		
Smilax (pg. 250)		
Ground cherry (pg. 68)		
Common chokecherry (pg. 154)		
Hawthorn (pg. 186)		
Smooth/staghorn sumac (pg. 188)		
Prickly pear (pg. 116)		
Bastard toadflax (pg. 44)		
Starry false Solomon's seal (pg. 38)		
Common pear (pg. 58)		
Maypop (pg. 50)		
Apple (pg. 190)		
Highbush cranberry (pg. 156)		
Common juniper (pg. 228)		
Russian olive (pg. 76)		
Callery pear (pg. 74)		
Mountain ash (pg. 86)		
Partridge berry (pg. 114)		
Chokeberry (pg. 282)		
Pawpaw (pg. 62)		
Autumn olive (pg. 160)		
Rose hip (pg. 140)		
Blackhaw, nannyberry (pg. 292)		
Japanese barberry (pg. 144)		
Hackberry, sugarberry (pg. 298)		
Tupelo, blackgum (pg. 214, 242)		
Northern spicebush (pg. 162)		
Persimmon (pg. 88)		

*Timing may vary by several weeks from the southern to the northern part of our area,
and also may vary from year to year depending on weather. Date ranges shown here are
an average; fruits in any given area may ripen a week or two earlier—or later—than shown.*

July	August	September	October	Winter

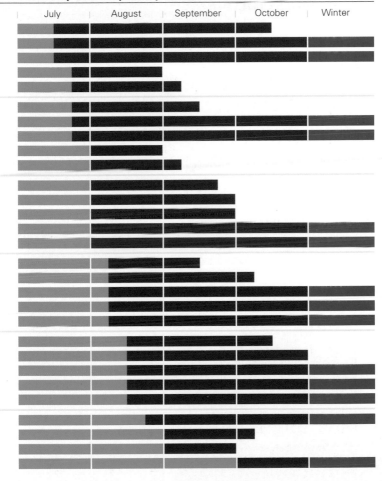

HOW TO USE THIS BOOK

1. When you find a plant with fruits, pay attention to **fruit color** first. Use the colored quarter-circles at the top corner of the left-hand pages to find the corresponding section.

SMALL WOODY SHRUB

2. Next, identify the **form of the plant**: is it a tender leafy plant, a shrub (small or large?), a vine or a tree? Flip through the color section until you find the proper form, using the icon at the top of the page.

3. Look through the **photos** in this section and see if you find similar fruits. If you can't, look in the color sections before and after the section you're in; if you are looking at a red fruit, but don't see anything like it, go to the orange section or to the purple section. Color judgment is subjective, and individual specimens may vary slightly, so you may have to look for the fruit in several color sections.

Mountain ash

It's also possible that you've found unripe fruit, and since this book shows fruits in the ripe stage, you might not be looking in the right color section. Most fruits are green when immature, ripening to a

Black raspberry

different color; but some pass through several colors before fully ripening. Black raspberries (pg. 258), for example, start out green and ripen to black; in between they turn yellow, salmon-orange, bright red, and purplish-red. Other fruits undergo similar transformations. Once you find something that looks similar— even if it's the wrong color — proceed to the next step.

4. Look at the **range map** icon at the top of the page to determine whether the plant is found in your area. Use these range maps as an approximation, as there are few official sources of information pertaining to wild plants, and no resource is all-inclusive.

ALTERNATE
LEAVES

5. When you find a photograph that appears similar to the fruit you've found (even if the color is not quite right), and the plant is the correct form, take a look at the **leaves** to see if they grow opposite one another on the stem, alternately on the stem, or in a whorl. This distinction is often the main key to properly identifying a plant.

6. Now read the full description, paying particular attention to any text that is in green; this color is used to point out key features that distinguish a plant from those with similar appearances. Also **study the "Compare" section**; here, you'll find information about plants that have similarities to the one pictured, along with page references for those which appear in this book. By following these references, you may sometimes find a photo showing the fruit you've found in a more ripened state; the description on that page will help you to identify the plant, even if you're looking at it in its unripe state.

SUMMER

7. To help determine when a fruit ripens, we've included a **season** icon at the top of the page. This will tell you the approximate season you're likely to find ripe berries or fruits and can help narrow down the possibilities when there are a number of look-alike fruits and berries.

8. Finally, the **thumb tab** at the top indicates whether a plant is toxic, not edible, edible, or delicious.

A species indicated as **toxic** has fruits that are highly poisonous and should not be eaten under any circumstances. The corresponding photo bears a skull and crossbones symbol for good reason; do not sample any part of a plant bearing this symbol. Species indicated as **not edible** bear fruit which, while not highly toxic, may cause sickness upon ingestion or have other negative side effects. Species indicated as **edible** bear fruits that are just that: edible. Some are bland but handy to know about as survival food, while others have a minor place in the forager's kitchen. Species indicated as **delicious** are the berries and fruits many people seek out. Blueberries, raspberries and chokecherries are just a few of the many delicious wild fruits found in Illinois, Iowa and Missouri. Unlike the fruits simply marked as edible, these are the best wild edibles the region has to offer.

Here's an example; follow along to see if you can identify this fruit.

The plant has fruit that is primarily red, and it is a large shrub (you can't see that in the photo above, but in the field, the form is obvious). Go to the red section of the book (starting on pg. 90), and flip to the beginning of the section that lists large shrubs (pg. 148).

LARGE
WOODY SHRUB

Twelve large shrubs (or large shrubs/small trees) are listed in the red section. Four of them (red elderberry, prickly ash, buttonbush and winged euonymus) can be eliminated, because the fruit doesn't look at all like this.

ALTERNATE
LEAVES

You notice that the leaves on this plant are alternate, spaced along the stem rather than across from one another. This eliminates bush honeysuckle and guelder rose/highbush cranberry. Six species remain as possibilities.

Examining the leaves more closely, you note that they have fine teeth. This eliminates autumn olive, northern spicebush and glossy buckthorn, whose leaves have smooth edges.

Three choices remain: common chokecherry, possumhaw/winterberry and Carolina buckthorn. First, double-check the range-maps for the species. Chokecherry (pg. 154) is found in the northern half of our region, and scattered in the southern half. You're in central

Iowa, so chokecherry is a possibility. You note that Carolina buckthorn (pg. 170) and possumhaw (pg. 158) are not in your region, so they are eliminated. Winterberry (pg. 158) remains a possibility; however, the description for winterberry mentions that the fruits grow from leaf axils, but the fruits on your plant are in a hanging cluster. Studying the text on the chokecherry page, it seems likely that you've found a chokecherry.

To confirm your identification, study the "Compare" text, to see what other plants resemble this one. Looking at the photos of black cherry (pg. 296) and pin cherry (pg. 178), you see that although the fruit is similar, those plants have leaves that are much narrower. In addition, your plant doesn't have any hairs on the midrib underneath, so it's not a black cherry; and the fruit on your plant is growing in a hanging cluster (a raceme) so it's not a pin cherry. The leaves do look like those of the serviceberry (pg. 208), but the fruit is not similar.

You've found a common chokecherry, a delicious wild edible fruit.

Once you've identified your wild fruit or berry, check the bottom of the page, as we've included a reference to our companion book, *Cooking with Wild Berries & Fruits of Illinois, Iowa and Missouri*, which includes delicious recipes, handy tips, and many different ways to put your newly found edible fruits and berries to use.

SMALL
WOODY SHRUB

ALTERNATE
COMPOUND
LEAVES

SUMMER

Common Name

Scientific name

HABITAT: General environment in which the plant is typically found in our area, including light and moisture requirements

GROWTH: The growth form of the plant in our area, ranging from small, tender plants, to vines, to small or large shrubs, to trees

LEAVES: Description of the plant's leaves, including leaf style and shape, arrangement on the plant, attachment to the main stem, and color of the leaves

FRUIT: Description of the fruit, including type (berry, pome, drupe or other), color, arrangement, appearance and edibility information

SEASON: When the plant bears ripe fruit in our area

COMPARE: Plants or fruits with similar attributes, including characteristics that differentiate them

NOTES: Interesting facts about the plant, including harvesting tips for edible plants, notes on other parts of the plant that may be edible, historical or modern-day medicinal uses, and miscellaneous tips and facts

TENDER
LEAFY PLANT

BASAL GROWTH
WITH PAIRED
LEAVES ON TOP

LATE SPRING
TO SUMMER

Celandine Poppy
–OR– Wood Poppy

Stylophorum diphyllum

HABITAT: Rich, moist deciduous woodlands and along stream edges; also found at the foot of bluffs and at the bottoms of ravines. It prefers shade, but will tolerate dappled sun. Celandine poppy is not widespread, but can form large colonies where present.

GROWTH: This native wildflower is a tender perennial, 12 to 18 inches in height. A hairy stem arises from a whorl of leaves at the base; paired leaves grow at the end of the stem. One to four yellow flowers, each with four petals, grow on long, hairy stemlets at the end of the main stem.

LEAVES: Large, multi-lobed leaves are up to 6 inches in length and almost as wide. Each leaf has five to seven lobes, each with smaller lobes along the edges. The two lobes closest to the stem are slightly separated from the group of lobes at the end of the leaf. Leaves are blue-green above and silvery below.

FRUIT: A football-shaped, densely hairy capsule, 1 to 1½ inches in length, replaces each flower. Capsules typically droop from the stemlets. Eventually, each capsule splits into 4 parts, dispersing the seeds. The plant also reproduces through rhizomes (underground root-bearing stems). The fruit is inedible.

SEASON: Bright yellow flowers appear in spring, followed by the fruiting capsule which is present from late spring through midsummer.

COMPARE: Greater celandine (*Chelidonium majus*) is an introduced plant with similar leaves and flowers, but the fruits resemble green beans and the leaves are not as deeply lobed. Several poppy species (*Papaver* spp.) have also escaped cultivation and are found occasionally in our area; the fruiting capsules are similar, but the leaves are much smaller and grow alternately along the length of the stem.

NOTES: The stems contain a yellow sap that has been used as a dye.

green = key identification feature

Flower

TENDER
LEAFY PLANT

ALTERNATE
LEAVES

SUMMER

Common False Solomon's Seal (unripe)

Maianthemum racemosum

HABITAT: This native plant is common and widespread in deciduous or mixed-wood forests. Also grows in waste ground.

GROWTH: The single stem usually grows in a zigzag fashion, bending slightly at each leaf axil; it may be up to 3 feet in length. When young, the stem is upright, but as the plant matures, it typically reclines until it is almost horizontal.

LEAVES: Bright green, shiny leaves are lance-shaped, with a sharp tip at the end; they are up to 8 inches long and about one-third as wide. Leaves are attached directly to the stem in an alternate arrangement, and feature deep parallel veins curving from base to tip.

FRUIT: Smooth, round berries grow in a long cluster at the end of the stem; each berry is about ⅛ inch across. Unripe berries are greenish with tiny purple blotches; ripe berries are deep red. The berries are bitter and generally regarded as inedible, although ripe berries may have been eaten by American Indians in the past (Sam Thayer).

SEASON: Unripe berries are present most of the summer; berries ripen in late summer.

COMPARE: Several plants in our area appear similar, but a closer look distinguishes them. Smooth Solomon's seal (pg. 216) bears fruit at the leaf axils rather than at the end of the stem. Starry false Solomon's seal (pg. 38) has a cluster of fruits at the end of the stem, but the plant is shorter, generally 2 feet or less, and the leaves are narrower. It tends to be more upright rather than reclining, and the fruits are pumpkin-shaped. Large-flowered belwort (*Uvularia grandiflora*, shown on pg. 16) is also short, about 2 feet tall; its leaves are perfoliate, and each stem bears a single triangular-shaped fruit.

NOTES: Another common name for this plant is feathery false lily of the valley. Some scientific texts list it as *Smilacina racemosa*.

green = key identification feature

Ripe berries

TENDER
LEAFY PLANT

ALTERNATE
LEAVES

SUMMER

Starry False Solomon's Seal (unripe)

Maianthemum stellatum

HABITAT: This native perennial inhabits cool, moist forests; often adjacent to streams, also found in sandy areas near marshes. Starry false Solomon's seal is often one of the first plants to grow after a forest fire.

GROWTH: A single stem grows from an underground rhizome (root-bearing stem) to a height of 1 to 2 feet. The plant arches somewhat, but is not droopy.

LEAVES: Lance-shaped leaves, up to 6 inches long and one-quarter as wide, grow alternately from the main stem, which appears to bend slightly at each leaf axil. Leaves attach directly to the stem, and are stiff and bluish-green, with prominent parallel veins; they are smooth on top and may be slightly hairy underneath.

FRUIT: A short raceme (a cluster of multiple fruits) of berries grows at the end of the stem. Unripe berries are green with dark red stripes, and are shaped rather like a small, squat pumpkin about 5/16 inch across. The berries ripen to dark red; they may retain subtle striping. The ripe berries are edible raw or cooked, but have a laxative effect if eaten when raw. They have a bittersweet flavor, and are reportedly high in vitamin C.

SEASON: Star-shaped white flowers, which give the plant its common name, appear from mid-spring to early summer. The green berries follow, and are present on the plant through most of the summer.

COMPARE: Please see the discussion of similar plants listed in common false Solomon's seal on pg. 36. Starry false Solomon's seal is most likely to be confused with common false Solomon's seal. Common false Solomon's seal is generally a larger plant, with more leaves and a larger number of berries in the terminal cluster; also, its berries are tiny and round, and are greenish speckled with purple when unripe.

NOTES: Starry false Solomon's seal is sometimes listed in references as *Smilacina stellata*. Ruffed grouse eat the ripe berries in autumn.

green = key identification feature

Ripe fruit

TENDER
LEAFY PLANT

ALTERNATE
LEAVES

SUMMER
THROUGH FALL

* see below

Jimsonweed

Datura stramonium, D. wrightii

HABITAT: Two jimsonweed species appear in our region: *Datura stramonium*, the common variety which is also called thorn apple; and *D. wrightii*, sacred jimsonweed (pictured at right), which in our area is scattered in only a few counties. Both are found in sunny pastures, waste ground, agricultural areas, and alongside rural roads.

GROWTH: An erect annual plant, generally 2 to 4 feet tall and bushy, with smooth, purplish stems that fork repeatedly. Each fork bears a white or pale lavender flower shaped like a deep, angular funnel with well-defined edges and sharp tips. The flowers have a pleasant scent, but all other parts of the plant have a foul odor, especially when crushed.

LEAVES: Dark green on top, lighter underneath, generally 4 to 6 inches long. Thorn apple leaves have pointed, irregular teeth and several lobes; they resemble an elongated maple or red-oak leaf. Sacred jimsonweed leaves typically have wavy edges and shallow or non-existent lobes.

FRUIT: Thorn-apple fruit is egg-shaped, about 2 inches long, growing upright from the fork of the stems. Fruit of sacred jimsonweed is more globe-like, up to 1½ inches, growing from the fork on a drooping stemlet. Both are covered in spiny prickles. Fruits are green when young, eventually turning brown and splitting to scatter seeds.

SEASON: Jimsonweed flowers throughout summer and into fall; fruits develop from the flower remnants throughout the season.

COMPARE: Bluestem pricklypoppy (*Argemone albiflora*), found occasionally in our area, has an egg-shaped spiny fruit growing upright on the stem, but leaves are prickly with multiple lobes; it is much less bushy.

NOTES: Thorn apple is non-native; it was noted in Jamestown, Virginia, during colonial days. Although sacred jimsonweed is a native plant, both it and thorn apple are considered pests in agricultural areas; cattle can be poisoned if they graze on the plants. Both contain scopolamine, atropine and hyoscyamine, powerful alkaloids that cause hallucinations, various physical difficulties, and, occasionally, death.

green = key identification feature   * combined range

TENDER
LEAFY PLANT

ALTERNATE
LEAVES

MID TO
LATE SUMMER

Apple-of-Peru –OR– **Shoo-fly** *Nicandra physalodes*

HABITAT: This non-native plant has escaped from gardens, and is found in disturbed areas, fields and waste ground, where it may spread and become weedy in appearance. It grows best in full to partial sun.

GROWTH: A branched, upright annual that may be up to 5 feet in height, although it is typically shorter; when large, it is usually very leafy. The main stem is slightly angled, and may have a purplish cast. Pale purple flowers grow at the ends of stems that originate in the leaf axils; the calyx (the green petal-like structure at the base of the flower) is sharply angled, net-veined and mottled with purple. After flowering, the calyx turns downward and closes around the flower remnant; a round berry forms inside the loose, husk-like calyx. Over time, both the calyx and the berry wither and turn brown, breaking open to release the seeds.

LEAVES: Oval leaves with a pointed tip, tapered base and large, irregular teeth grow alternately on grooved petioles (stemlets); leaves are 3 to 8 inches in length and half as wide. They are medium-green on top, and often have a scattering of tiny black dots; undersides are paler.

FRUIT: A round, many-seeded berry, ½ inch across, grows inside the papery husk, which has five sharply angled edges that end in pointed tips at the base. The berry is green during development, turning brown and withering away on maturity. It is often regarded as mildly toxic, and should not be eaten.

SEASON: Apple-of-Peru flowers in mid to late summer; green fruits develop in late summer, withering to brown in fall.

COMPARE: Ground cherries (pg. 68) have similar round berries inside papery husks, but their husks are not as sharply angled as those of apple-of-Peru, and they lack the pointed tips at the base; also, ground cherry husks are not mottled with purple.

NOTES: The flowers last a single day before withering; they are reputed to repel insects.

green = key identification feature

42

Berry inside calyx

TENDER
LEAFY PLANT

ALTERNATE
LEAVES

MID TO LATE
SUMMER

Bastard Toadflax
–OR– Comandra

Comandra umbellata

HABITAT: Meadows, grasslands, prairies, edges, and dry, open woods; occasionally found in mixed evergreen forests. It requires plenty of sunlight and good drainage.

GROWTH: This small, erect native perennial is typically 4 to 8 inches high, but can reach 16 inches; it often grows in large colonies. Stems are light green and smooth, and woody near the base. Although it is able to photosynthesize, it also uses suckers (shoots) to attach itself to the roots of other plants, stealing water and nutrients from them.

LEAVES: The thick, alternate leaves are 1 to 2 inches long and about one-quarter as wide. They are attached directly to the stem or by a very short petiole (stemlet). Leaves are light grayish-green and smooth, with smooth edges that may appear slightly turned under. Some leaf tips may have a slight reddish tinge. The midvein is prominent on the underside of the leaf.

FRUIT: A green drupe about ¼ inch across, with a long, reddish crown at the end; the fruit seems large in proportion to the plant. The fruits are sweet when young, but have thin flesh with a slightly oily texture. They make a decent trailside nibble, but are not worth seeking out. Later in the season, the fruits turn brown and become unappetizing.

SEASON: Bastard toadflax produces white flowers in late spring through midsummer; fruits ripen in mid to late summer.

COMPARE: The leaves and growth habit of bastard toadflax resemble true toadflax (*Linaria* spp.), but *Linaria* don't produce drupes.

NOTES: The flower stamens have small hairs at their bases, giving the plant its species name, *Comandra* (a combination of the Greek words for "hair" and "man"). *Umbellata* refers to the flat-topped, umbrella-like flower clusters.

green = key identification feature

TENDER PLANT
(SUBSHRUB)

BASAL
GROWTH

MID TO LATE
SUMMER

• see below

Yucca –OR– **Adam's Needle**

Yucca filamentosa

HABITAT: Sandy, sunny areas including prairies, waste ground, roadsides, open woods, and railroad beds. Adam's needle is native to the southeastern United States, and is grown in our area as a showy garden specimen; it has escaped cultivation and is found occasionally in the wild in our area. Some texts refer to this plant as *Y. smalliana;* which is more commonly an alternate name for weak-leaf yucca (*Y. flaccida*).

GROWTH: Adam's needle appears to be a tender plant, but is actually a perennial subshrub. The spiky, evergreen leaves grow in a tight cluster, and the thick flowering stalk arises from the center of the leaves. The flowering stalk has multiple branches and may be up to 6 feet in height.

LEAVES: Stiff, sword-shaped leaves grow in a basal form. Leaves are slightly rough in texture, with a blue-green color; they are up to 2½ feet in length, with bases up to 2 inches wide. Tips are sharply pointed; leaf edges are smooth but the leaves often have whitish thread-like fibers curling away from the edges.

FRUIT: The lumpy, rounded green fruit has two distinct lobes; it is up to 2½ inches in length and half as wide. In fall, the pod darkens and splits into three parts to release its seeds. The pods are inedible.

SEASON: Showy white flowers, which are pleasantly fragrant, bloom in late spring through midsummer (depending on location); the green seed pods are formed in mid to late summer.

COMPARE: Soapweed (*Y. glauca*) is a related plant that also occasionally escapes cultivation in our area; it inhabits the same areas as Adam's needle. Its leaves are very similar to Adam's needle but may be longer and thinner; the flowers grow on the central flowering stalk rather than on lateral branches. Fruits are similar in appearance.

NOTES: In spring, before the flowers develop, the central stalk can be cooked and eaten like asparagus. The flowers may be breaded and fried; they are also edible raw, but may have an unpleasant after taste.

green = key identification feature

* specific locations not available

Adam's needle plant in flower

Adam's needle fruit

WOODY
VINE

ALTERNATE
COMPOUND
LEAVES

SUMMER

Eastern Poison Ivy

Toxicodendron radicans

HABITAT: This native woody vine grows throughout our area, and is found in a variety of habitats. It thrives in moist areas with moderate sun such as road ditches, open woodlands, fencelines, swampy areas and stream banks, but it may also be found in agricultural fields, sandy areas and disturbed sites.

GROWTH: A woody perennial vine that climbs trees, fences, posts and anything else it encounters, attaching itself to the supporting structure with thick, hairy stems (the hairs are actually aerial roots). Stems are reddish to gray. Eastern poison ivy may also grow as a shrub, or even a ground-hugging plant; it also hybridizes with western poison ivy (*T. rydbergii*, pg. 306), a low-growing form.

LEAVES: Three-part leaves grow on the ends of long, pale green stalks attached alternately to the main stem. The petiole (stemlet) of the middle leaflet is longer than those of the side leaflets. Leaves of eastern poison ivy are often up to 8 inches in length, much larger than those of western poison ivy. Edges have large, irregular teeth. Leaves turn yellow to reddish in fall, often with a blotchy appearance.

FRUIT: The round, ridged berries are ⅛ to ³⁄₁₆ inch across and green when immature, ripening to whitish. Berries of eastern poison ivy grow from leaf axils in loose clusters; the clusters are usually large and abundant. Berries, and all other parts of the plant, are toxic and may cause a painful rash if touched.

SEASON: Green berries are present much of the summer, ripening to white in the fall.

COMPARE: Western poison ivy is a low-growing plant, with smaller leaves and fewer berries. Both are toxic.

NOTES: Eastern poison ivy is common throughout most of our region. It is included here, in the green section of the book, because its abundant green berries are prominent most of the summer, and pose a threat to inquisitive children. See pg. 306 for more information on poison ivy.

green = key identification feature

Aerial roots on stem

TENDER
VINE

ALTERNATE
LEAVES

LATE SUMMER
THROUGH FALL

Passionflower –OR– Maypop

Passiflora incarnata

HABITAT: This native vine is found in sunny locations such as field edges, fencerows, unmowed pastures, railroad embankments, streambanks, waste ground and ditches; it prefers sandy soil and full sun.

GROWTH: A non-woody vine up to 30 feet in length, passionflower uses tendrils to twine itself around other plants, fences and buildings, often reaching a height of 10 feet or more; if a supporting structure is not present, it will sprawl along the ground. It spreads very aggressively. Stems are smooth or slightly hairy. Distinctive purple, frilly flowers, 2 to 3 inches across, grow throughout the summer from the leaf axils.

LEAVES: Palmately lobed leaves with three divisions (occasionally five) grow alternately on the vine on medium-length petioles (stemlets); two sticky tendrils are present where the leaf attaches to the petiole. Leaves are 3 to 6 inches across with pointed tips and finely toothed edges; the top surface is dark green and smooth, the underside paler.

FRUIT: Egg-shaped berries, 2 to 3 inches in length, are green and smooth at first, becoming yellowish and wrinkly with age. When cut open, the fruit reveals a thick, spongy white rind filled with seeds, each surrounded by translucent, gel-like pulp. The seedy pulp is edible, with a sweet-tart flavor; it is often juiced, but can be eaten raw or cooked.

SEASON: Flowers are present from spring through summer; fruits ripen from late summer through early fall.

COMPARE: Yellow passionflower (pg. 224) is a similar vine, but its leaves are less deeply lobed; its flowers are yellow, and ripe fruits are very small and bluish.

NOTES: Passionflower fruits burst with a 'pop' when stepped on, possibly accounting for the common name. Ripe maypops may be green or yellowish, but they are heavier than underripe fruit of the same size (Sam Thayer). Underripe maypops can be left on a counter to ripen, but flavor is best when vine-ripened. Herbalists prepare a sedative from the leaves; the fruits may have a sedative effect when eaten.

green = key identification feature

Cut-open maypop

TENDER
VINE

ALTERNATE
LEAVES

LATE SUMMER
THROUGH FALL

Wild Cucumber
–OR– Balsam Apple

Echinocystis lobata

HABITAT: Stream banks, moist thickets and woods, roadsides, swamp edges. Generally found in sunny locations.

GROWTH: A native, non-woody vining plant with coiled tendrils; nodes are sometimes hairy. Grows rapidly, and can reach 25 feet in length.

LEAVES: Alternating leaves, somewhat resembling maple leaves, grow on long petioles (stemlets); each typically has five distinct triangular lobes, but may have as few as three or as many as seven lobes.

FRUIT: A pulpy green berry-like fruit with a firm skin (called a *pepo*), 1 to 2 inches long, roughly egg-shaped, sometimes with blunt ends, grows from the leaf node. The fruit has supple, spiny prickles overall. Eventually the fruit dries out and turns brown, splitting open at the end to disperse its four seeds. The fruit is inedible.

SEASON: Wild cucumber blooms in mid to late summer, producing a profusion of lacy white flowers that may blanket the surrounding vegetation; fruits are present from late summer through early fall.

COMPARE: Wild grapes (pg. 196) are vining plants with similar leaves, but the fruit is entirely different, resembling the familiar commercial grape. Guadeloupe cucumber (*Melothria pendula*) has similar leaves and growth form, but the fruits are small, smooth, tough-skinned pepos that lack prickles. Bur cucumber (*Sicyos angulatus*) has a spiny green fruit that is not egg-shaped but rather has many points, looking something like a small, prickly, three-dimensional star ornament.

NOTES: The roots of wild cucumber have been used medicinally, to treat ailments including headache, stomach problems, rheumatism and even love-sickness. According to *Native American Ethnobotany* (Daniel E. Moerman; Timber Press), the seeds were used as beads by American Indian peoples.

green = key identification feature

SMALL
WOODY SHRUB

ALTERNATE
LEAVES

LATE SPRING
TO SUMMER

• see below

Gooseberry (green stage)

Ribes spp.

HABITAT: Three native gooseberry species are found in our area: Missouri (*Ribes missouriense*), prickly (*R. cynosbati*), and smooth or swamp (*R. hirtellum*). Gooseberries inhabit thickets and tangled areas, scrubby shelterbelts, rocky areas, and rich, moist woods, especially those along rivers or ponds.

GROWTH: An arching shrub about 3 feet high. Missouri and prickly goose-berry stems have scattered small bristles on young and mature stems. Mature stems of smooth gooseberries have small hairs but no bristles; young stems have scattered small bristles. Leaf nodes of all three have one to three sharp thorns.

LEAVES: Attached alternately to the stem by a petiole (stemlet). Each leaf has three to five distinct lobes, resembling a rounded maple leaf. Leaf undersides are slightly hairy on smooth and Missouri gooseberries; prickly gooseberry leaves have more hairs on the undersides.

FRUIT: The ¼- to ½-inch round berry grows singly or in clusters of two or three. Prickly gooseberry fruits have soft prickles, either overall or around the half of the fruit closest to the stem; fruits of the others are smooth. All have distinct stripes that run longitudinally; a flower remnant, called a pigtail, is present at the end of the berry. Gooseberries are green when young, ripening to red, purple, or black.

SEASON: Fruit is green but edible in late spring through midsummer.

COMPARE: Currant shrubs (pgs. 134 and 266) resemble gooseberry shrubs, but fruit is borne in racemes (long clusters of multiple fruits). Horse nettle (pg. 66) bears **toxic** green berries on prickly stems, but it is a shorter plant, not a shrub, with leaves that resemble oak, not maple.

NOTES: Green gooseberries are rich in pectin, and are used primarily for jam, jelly and pie. Taste a few before harvesting; they will be sour, but if they are too astringent, let them mature a bit longer before picking. When the fruits ripen (pgs. 136, 202 and 264), they are excellent in baked desserts, sauces and other dishes.

green = key identification feature

* combined range

Missouri gooseberry

Prickly gooseberry

TREE

OPPOSITE
LEAVES

MID TO LATE
SUMMER

* see below

Princess Tree

Paulownia tomentosa

HABITAT: This non-native tree has escaped cultivation, and is increasingly found in the wild, where it is sometimes considered a weedy, invasive tree. It prefers areas with deep, moist, well-drained soil, but is tolerant of drought and pollution; it is found in woodland edges and disturbed forests, along railroad beds and streambanks, and on rocky slopes.

GROWTH: This large tree can grow up to 12 feet in a season, and can reach a height of 50 feet, with equal spread; wild specimens tend to be smaller. Bark is grayish-brown with narrow fissures; twigs are brown or green with numerous lenticels (breathing pores). In spring, it produces hundreds of pale lavender flowers before the leaves develop, making a striking display.

LEAVES: Heart-shaped leaves, as much as 12 inches in length and about two-thirds as wide, grow oppositely on long, smooth petioles (stem-lets). Some trees have leaves with several sharply pointed lobes on the sides, while others have smooth edges with no lobes. Leaves are dark green on top and paler below, and lightly fuzzy or rough on both sides; edges are untoothed. Veins are prominent on the undersides.

FRUIT: The fruit, a dry capsule, looks a bit like an elongated green acorn with a loose, frilly brown cap. When fully developed, it is 1½ to 2 inches long and half as wide, with a broad top and a pointed tip; the hard shell is green, with a rough, sticky texture. It is not edible.

SEASON: Developed green fruits are present in mid to late summer; in fall, they turn brown and split open, spilling over 1,000 seeds per fruit. Small brown flower buds follow and are present through winter.

COMPARE: Catalpa (*Catalpa* spp.) somewhat resemble the princess tree, but catalpa fruits are long, thin, hanging pods.

NOTES: Paulownia wood is prized for carving in China and Japan. Some sources say that in its native China, a princess tree is planted when a baby girl is born. The tree matures with the child; when she reaches the age of marriage, its wood is used to carve items for her dowry.

green = key identification feature   * specific MO and IL locations not available

TREE

ALTERNATE
LEAVES

MID TO LATE
SUMMER

* see below

Common Pear

Pyrus communis and others

HABITAT: This is the common orchard pear, which has escaped cultivation and is found in scattered spots in the wild; other species, such as the sand pear (*P. pyrifolia*), may also be found. Pears may be "planted" by anglers, hunters or picnickers who throw out a core after eating a commercial pear, so they are found near boat launches, parks and hiking trails. Pears do best in sunny areas with rich, moist, well-drained soil.

GROWTH: A medium to large tree, with a straight trunk and an open, spreading crown. Unlike orchard pears, which are grafted onto shorter stock to make picking easy, wild pears grow from seed, and tend to be taller than their domestic cousins. The trunk has furrowed grayish bark. Branches are reddish-brown to grayish; most are smooth, with visible gray lenticels (breathing pores), but side branches often have wrinkled bark or are knobby-looking. Pear trees have no thorns.

LEAVES: Glossy, thick, leathery leaves, up to 4 inches in length and two-thirds as wide, grow alternately or in clusters on long yellowish-green petioles (stemlets). Leaves have pointed tips and are broadest near the base or below the midpoint; they often fold in slightly along the midline. Edges are finely serrated, and may appear wavy.

FRUIT: A greenish to yellowish pome, generally 1 to 2 inches across; the skin is rough, with fine brown patches or tiny dots. Pears grow on a thick stemlet and have a crown on the bottom. Unlike commercial pears, wild pears have little or no neck; they often grow with the crown end up, looking like a large, rough-skinned crabapple. Wild pears are generally firmer than domestic pears, but taste similar.

SEASON: Wild pears ripen in mid to late summer.

COMPARE: Crabapples (pg. 174) are similar trees, but leaves taper at both ends, and are thinner and rougher than pear leaves; branches have thorns. Callery pears (pg. 74) have smaller fruits that are bronze in color.

NOTES: Wild pears may fall off the tree before fully ripe, but will ripen if left on the countertop for a few days.

green = key identification feature   * specific locations not available

TREE

ALTERNATE
LEAVES

LATE SUMMER
TO FALL

* see below

Osage Orange
–OR– **Hedge Apple**

Maclura pomifera

HABITAT: Open sunny areas and rich bottomlands are prime habitat. This native tree is also found in pastures and along fence rows, and occasionally along riverbanks.

GROWTH: A deciduous tree, up to 40 feet high with approximately equal width. Osage orange has many branches, and the foliage is dense, giving the appearance of a very solid tree. The trunk has brown bark with strong vertical fissures and orange patches. Only female trees bear fruit, and not until they are about 10 years old.

LEAVES: Bright green oblong leaves, 3 to 7 inches long, grow alternately on the stems. Leaves are smooth and glossy, with a rounded base and sharply pointed tip; although the edges are smooth, the leaves tend to curl upwards along the edges and may appear wavy. Half-inch-long thorns grow at leaf nodules. If a leaf or thorn is pulled off, milky sap will appear on the stem (careful; the sap may irritate the skin).

FRUIT: The pebbly-textured, leathery sphere, 4 to 6 inches across, consists of a pithy core surrounded by abundant small seeds. The fruit is light green with fine hairs when immature, ripening to yellowish-green with a mild orange scent. Osage orange fruit is generally regarded as mildly toxic; sap from the fruit can cause skin irritation.

SEASON: Osage orange blooms in early summer; the large, round fruit grows throughout summer, ripening in late summer to fall.

COMPARE: Nothing in our area resembles the fruit of the Osage orange.

NOTES: Some people place Osage orange fruits around the foundation of the house, in the basement or near windows and doors to repel insects. The fruit also provides food for squirrels, who shred it and strip the slimy husk off the seeds before eating them. Osage orange is named after the Osage, an American Indian tribe that inhabited the tree's native range in Oklahoma and portions of the surrounding states.

green = key identification feature   * specific IA locations not available

Mature fruit and thorns

TREE

ALTERNATE LEAVES

LATE SUMMER TO EARLY FALL

Pawpaw

Asimina triloba

HABITAT: Areas with deep, rich soil including bottomlands, stream and river banks, floodplains, ravines and ditches. Pawpaw prefers sun, but also grows in shady areas; it produces the most fruit in sunny areas.

GROWTH: This native tree can attain heights up to 40 feet, but is usually much shorter; it may appear shrub-like. It often grows in a "patch" or thicket, with larger central trees towering over the smaller surrounding upstarts. Bark is smooth and light brown, often with light-colored splotches; it has numerous small, wart-like lenticels (breathing pores). Twigs are downy when young, becoming smooth as they mature.

LEAVES: Thick, bright green leaves grow alternately on **short petioles (stemlets)**; they tend to **cluster towards the ends of the branches.** Leaves are oblong, with tapered bases and a pointed tip; they are up to 11 inches in length and about one-third as wide, **broadest above the midpoint.** They have smooth edges and numerous prominent veins.

FRUIT: Green, smooth-skinned fruits grow singly or in clusters on short, thick stemlets along the branches. Fruits are typically oblong and somewhat **irregularly shaped**; they are 2 to 6 inches in length. When ripe, the fruits become softer to the touch, and may become pale yellowish-green flecked with brown. The interior of the ripe fruit is creamy yellow, with 8 to 13 flat, oval seeds. The fruit is a prime edible, tasting similar to a banana with pineapple and apricot overtones; it can be eaten raw, or used in baked goods. It may cause stomach upset or intestinal problems in some people. The seeds should not be eaten.

SEASON: Pawpaw fruits are present much of the summer, but don't ripen until late summer to early fall.

COMPARE: Corkwood (pg. 70) has similar slender trunks and grows in thickets, but its leaves are narrower; fruits are small yellowish drupes.

NOTES: Pawpaw fruit is rich in vitamin C, potassium and iron. It was a dietary staple of American Indians and early settlers, and was much favored by the Lewis and Clark expedition members.

green = key identification feature

Leaves

TENDER
LEAFY PLANT

OPPOSITE
LEAVES

MID TO LATE
SUMMER

Mayapple –or– Mandrake

Podophyllum peltatum

HABITAT: Rich, dappled woodlands with loamy soil. This native plant grows in shade, but requires moderate sun to produce fruit.

GROWTH: A smooth green stem grows from the underground rhizome (root-bearing stem) to a height of 12 to 18 inches; a large palmately lobed leaf grows at the top of the stem. Some plants have a forked stem, with a large leaf on top of each fork; only forked plants will flower and produce fruit. Mayapples usually grow in large colonies.

LEAVES: Each deep green, palmately lobed leaf is 8 to 10 inches wide and has five to nine lobes with toothy edges; the overall outline is a circle. Plants with a single stem have one leaf, while those with a forked stem have two. A colony of mayapple plants resembles a miniature woodland café, with the leaves serving as patio umbrellas.

FRUIT: In spring, a single flower grows on a long stemlet from the fork in the stem. An egg-shaped green berry appears after the flower, and matures slowly over the summer; full-sized berries can be up to 2 inches long. When the leaves start dying, the plant often falls to the ground with the unripe green fruit still attached; foragers typically gather the fruit at that time and let it ripen to yellow on the countertop. Fully ripe berries are edible raw but are usually cooked or juiced; they have a lemony, tropical taste, and numerous small seeds like those of cantaloupe. Caution is essential because *seeds, unripe berries and all other parts of the plant are toxic.* As with all wild edibles, eat only a small portion until you are sure you won't have an adverse reaction. Before picking or eating any mayapples, it's best to get the guidance of a forager who is experienced in judging ripeness of the fruit.

SEASON: Berries ripen to yellow from mid to late summer.

COMPARE: Goldenseal (pg. 100) has a has a similar growth habit, with a forked stem topped by a large leaf; however, the fruits are dissimilar.

NOTES: The rhizome is extremely toxic, but is used medicinally to treat genital warts; studies suggest it may also have anti-cancer properties.

green = key identification feature

64

Unripe mayapple berry on plant (all parts of the plant are toxic at this stage)

Ripe mayapple berry

TENDER
LEAFY PLANT

ALTERNATE
LEAVES

SUMMER
THROUGH FALL

• see below

Horse Nettle (several)   *Solanum carolinense* and others

HABITAT: Three types of horse nettle are native to our area: Carolina (*Solanum carolinense*, pictured at right), western (*S. dimidiatum*) and white (*S. elaeagnifolium*, also called silverleaf nightshade). The latter two are in Illinois and Missouri, but not Iowa. Horse nettles grow in agricultural areas, pastures, waste ground and disturbed sites; also along roads, fences, trails and railroad grades. They thrive in sunny areas.

GROWTH: Horse nettle is an erect, branching herbaceous plant that is typically about 2 feet tall, although it can grow to 3 feet. Its hairy stems are armed with sharp spines that can stick in the skin and break off, making it despised by gardeners. Carolina horse nettle flowers are white or pale lavender; flowers of the other two are purple.

LEAVES: Alternate, covered with fine, starry hairs on both surfaces. Leaves are irregularly lobed and shaped like a rounded oak leaf; they are up to 7 inches in length and are attached to the stem by short petioles (stemlets). The midribs and parts of the veins have small but sharp thorns. Leaves of white horse nettle have a silvery cast.

FRUIT: A round, many-seeded berry, up to 1 inch in diameter at maturity. Fruits are borne in drooping clusters on a leafless stem. Immature berries are bright green with darker, somewhat blotchy stripes. Green fruit is toxic, and is sometimes blamed for cattle deaths. When ripe, the glossy yellow-to-orangeish berries resemble small, yellow tomatoes. Ripe berries are reported to be toxic in large quantities.

SEASON: Flowers appear in late spring, and bloom all summer. Fruits develop a week or two later, and can be found through early fall.

COMPARE: Horse nettle resembles eastern black nightshade (pg. 248), which has similar flowers, fruits and leaf shape. However, nightshade has no spines; its fruits are much smaller, and are black when mature.

NOTES: Despite its common name, horse nettle is a member of the nightshade family, not the nettle family (*Urtica* sp.). It is resistant to herbicides and is considered a noxious agricultural pest.

green = key identification feature   * combined range

Ripe fruit

TENDER
LEAFY PLANT

ALTERNATE
LEAVES

MID TO
LATE SUMMER

* see below

Ground Cherry (several) *Physalis heterophylla and others*

HABITAT: Fields, slopes, rocky areas and waste ground; often found along fences, streams and railroad grades. They are native to our area.

GROWTH: A very leafy plant, 1 to 4 feet in height. Depending on variety, it grows as a perennial from **underground rhizomes** (root-bearing stems), or as an annual from a **taproot**. In our area, perennials include the clammy (*Physalis heterophylla*), Virginia (*P. virginiana*) and smooth (*P. longifolia*) ground cherry; annuals include downy (*P. pubescens*), strawberry-tomato (*P. grisea*) and cutleaf (*P. angulata*) ground cherry.

LEAVES: Alternate, on short to medium petioles (stemlets). Leaf shapes are highly variable; leaves of some species have large, irregular teeth, but others are smooth-edged or slightly wavy.

FRUIT: A round, many-seeded berry, ½ to ¾ inch across, is enclosed in a **ribbed husk** that hangs from a leaf axil or stem fork; husks of most species have **10 equally spaced ribs** that may be subtle. Berries of the listed species are yellow to orangish when ripe. *Unripe berries and all other parts of the plant, including the papery husk, are toxic.*

SEASON: **Yellow** bell-shaped flowers, generally with dark spots inside the base, are present all summer; the berries ripen in mid to late summer.

COMPARE: Three non-native ground cherries are occasionally found in our area as escapees from cultivation. Tomatillo (*P. philadelphica*) has edible 1-inch-wide berries that fill the husk completely. The inedible Chinese lantern (*P. alkekengi*) has an orange husk. Apple-of-Peru (pg. 42) has an inedible green berry; its husk has very sharply angled edges.

NOTES: Key features help identify individual species. Clammy ground cherry has sticky hairs overall; leaves are wide with large, rounded teeth. Virginia and smooth have narrow leaves that often lack teeth; those of smooth ground cherry often have an asymmetric base, and the stem is grooved. Downy and strawberry-tomato husks have five sharply distinct ribs; downy have heart-shaped leaves, while those of strawberry-tomato are narrower. Cutleaf has dark veins on the husk.

green = key identification feature   * combined range

Ripe ground cherries

Clammy
ground cherry

Husks shown contain
unripe green berries
(all parts of the plant
are toxic at this stage)

Smooth
ground cherry

LARGE SHRUB
OR SMALL TREE

ALTERNATE
LEAVES

MID TO LATE
SUMMER

Corkwood

Leitneria floridana

HABITAT: Wet areas, including swamps, shady marshes, moist thickets, low woodlands and along the edges of ponds and streams. In coastal areas of the southeast, it is found in areas with both fresh and brackish water. It is uncommon, but grows in large colonies when it is found.

GROWTH: A large native shrub or small tree, corkwood reproduces by suckers and typically forms dense colonies. It has smooth, reddish-brown bark with tan or gray lenticels (breathing pores); young branches are pale and downy. The trunk is slender and typically unbranched to about head height. Corkwood can grow up to 20 feet in height, but is usually shorter.

LEAVES: Narrow, elliptic leaves that taper on both ends grow alternately on long, thick, pale petioles (stemlets), and tend to cluster at the ends of the trunk. Leaves are thick and leathery, up to 7 inches in length and one-quarter as wide; edges are smooth. They are deep green and somewhat glossy on top; undersides are paler and hairy, with prominent veins. Leaves remain green into late fall.

FRUIT: Leathery, irregularly shaped yellow drupes, typically about 1 inch long and one-third as wide, develop in small clusters on short branches along the top of the trunk; the fruits are narrower at the base and often bulge slightly near the midpoint. They are not edible.

SEASON: Inconspicuous greenish-gray flowers appear in early spring, before the leaves appear; fruits develop in late spring, changing from greenish to yellow by mid to late summer.

COMPARE: Pawpaw (pg. 62) has similar slender trunks and also grows in thickets, but its leaves are wider, especially toward the tip; pawpaw fruits are large and pale green.

NOTES: Corkwood gets its name from its soft, lightweight wood, which is naturally buoyant. Stem sections have been used as floats for fishing nets, and the fruits as bobbers. Wetland drainage has eliminated much of corkwood's habitat, and it is considered endangered.

green = key identification feature

Lenticels on trunk

TREE

ALTERNATE
COMPOUND
LEAVES

MID TO
LATE SUMMER

Western Soapberry

Sapindus saponaria

HABITAT: Well-drained areas such as edges of forests, fields and stream banks; also found on rocky hillsides or in bottomlands. An adaptable tree that can tolerate infertile soil as well as wind, drought and heat.

GROWTH: This native tree can grow to 50 feet in height, although it is usually much shorter; the crown is full, and some branches may bend low enough that the leaves almost touch the ground. The trunk has reddish-brown bark with raised, gray plates that fall off in large pieces. Soapberry produces suckers and may grow in colonies.

LEAVES: Compound leaves, 12 to 18 inches in length with 4 to 10 pairs of leaflets, grow alternately; a terminal leaflet is often present. Leaflets are 2 to 3 inches in length, with smooth edges and a sharply pointed tip; they are bright green, smooth and glossy above, paler and fuzzy below. Leaflets are asymmetrical; the half towards the branch tip is broader than the half closer to the trunk and the leaflet is usually deeply curved, resembling a crescent moon. Leaves turn yellow in fall.

FRUIT: Round, golden-yellow drupes grow in branched racemes (long clusters of multiple fruits) at the tips of branches; as they ripen, the skin becomes wrinkled and translucent. Each fruit is ½ to ¾ inch across, and usually contains one dark-brown seed. Fruits may persist over winter, darkening to black. The fruits contain saponin, a bitter substance that is toxic in large doses; they should not be eaten.

SEASON: Creamy yellow flowers profusely adorn the tree in late spring. Fruits follow, and ripen to golden-yellow in mid to late summer.

COMPARE: Soapberry is often mistaken for chinaberry (*Melia azedarach*), which grows in scattered locations in Missouri, but chinaberry's leaves are twice or thrice compound, with an overall triangular outline. Soapberry leaves resemble those of walnut (*Juglans* spp.) or hickory (*Carya* spp.), but hickory and walnut produce nuts, not drupes.

NOTES: The fruits contain saponin, a foaming compound that has been used as a soap substitute. It may cause an allergic reaction in some.

green = key identification feature

TREE ALTERNATE LATE SUMMER
LEAVES TO EARLY FALL

* see below

Callery Pear

Pyrus calleryana

HABITAT: Callery pear has been widely planted as an ornamental tree, and is increasingly found in the wild, where it is considered a pest tree in some areas. It is tolerant of a wide variety of habitats, and is found in urban woodlots, abandoned fields, industrial parklands and disturbed areas, where its seeds were likely deposited by birds.

GROWTH: A medium tree, up to 40 feet in height, with a straight trunk and a pyramid-shaped crown. The trunk has furrowed gray or gray-brown bark. Branches are reddish-brown to gray; most are smooth, with gray lenticels (breathing pores). Branches are often armed with thorns.

LEAVES: Glossy, thick, leathery leaves, up to 3 inches in length and two-thirds as wide, grow alternately or in clusters on long pale petioles (stemlets). Leaves have pointed tips and are broadest near the base; they often fold in slightly along the midline. Edges are finely serrated, and may appear wavy. Leaves turn scarlet, yellow or purple in fall.

FRUIT: A round, bronze-colored pome with tiny, light speckles and rough skin; the fruit is generally about ½ inch across. Callery pears grow on a thick, orangish stemlet and have a small crown on the bottom. They often grow with the crown end up, looking like a speckled bronze crabapple. Callery pears are edible but too small and hard to eat out-of-hand; they can be juiced, puréed or stewed.

SEASON: Callery pears produce strongly scented white flowers in spring; the fruits follow, and are ripe in late summer to early fall.

COMPARE: Crabapples (pg. 174) are similar in growth form, but the fruits are not speckled; crabapple leaves tend to taper at both ends, and are much thinner and rougher than Callery pear leaves. Common pears (pg. 58) have larger fruits that are greenish or yellowish in color, with brown blotches or fine dots.

NOTES: When picked before a frost, the flesh of Callery pears is hard, but it softens when cooked. They are not as tasty as common pears. Callery pears are often referred to as Bradford pears.

green = key identification feature   * specific IA and IL locations not available

EDIBLE

TREE

ALTERNATE
LEAVES

LATE SUMMER
TO EARLY FALL

* see below

Russian Olive
– OR– **Oleaster**

Elaeagnus angustifolia

HABITAT: An introduced plant, Russian olive is found in floodplain forests, irrigation ditches, and grasslands. It also grows along railroad grades, roads and fence lines. It tolerates seasonal flooding, but also survives in areas that suffer occasional drought. Prefers sun, but will grow in dappled shade. A very adaptable plant.

GROWTH: A small tree, sometimes appearing as a large shrub; up to 20 feet tall, often with a rounded, spreading crown. Branches are silvery when young, maturing to reddish brown; some have small thorns.

LEAVES: Lance-shaped leaves are grayish-green above; the undersides are silvery. They grow alternately and are generally 2 to 4 inches long and one-quarter as wide, with smooth margins and a well-defined midrib. Leaves are rough-textured on both sides.

FRUIT: The oval drupe, about ½ inch long, is yellow when ripe, and is covered with fine silvery scales. Fruits grow abundantly along the stems from short, scaly stemlets. The fruit, although somewhat dry, is sweet, and can be eaten raw, pulped to make fruit leather, or cooked for jam. It is quite astringent when underripe.

SEASON: Pleasantly scented yellow flowers appear in spring; the fruit follows and ripens in late summer to early fall.

COMPARE: Autumn olive (pg. 160) has a similar silvery appearance, but its leaves are wider, roughly one-half as wide as they are long. Fruits of autumn olive are rounder and smaller, and are red with silvery scales; they are also more juicy than those of Russian olive. Autumn olive usually has fewer thorns, sometimes no thorns at all.

NOTES: Russian olive was widely planted during the 1800s in disturbed areas; it is good for stabilizing embankments. It also offers cover and food for wildlife. Nonetheless, it is considered invasive in some areas because it shades out native understory plants and spreads rapidly.

green = key identification feature   * specific IA locations not available

TENDER
LEAFY PLANT

OPPOSITE
LEAVES

MID TO
LATE SUMMER

• see below

Horse Gentian
–OR– **Feverwort** (several)   *Triosteum aurantiacum* and others

HABITAT: Rocky and wooded areas, especially with rich soil; thickets; wooded ridgetops. Prefers areas with dappled sun.

GROWTH: An erect, unbranched, native perennial, 2 to 4 feet in height. Stems are covered with fine, long hairs; leaves are slightly hairy on the edges and the undersides.

LEAVES: Large, oval leaves, up to 8 inches long and one-half as wide, grow oppositely in pairs; the edges are smooth and the leaf terminates in a sharp tip. Leaf pairs grow in intervals along the stem; each pair is rotated 90° from the previous pair. Three varieties inhabit our area. Early horse gentian (*Triosteum aurantiacum*, pictured at right) and yellow-flowered horse gentian (*T. angustifolium*) have leaves that are distinct from one another, connected to the stem by a tapering neck. Perfoliate horse gentian (*T. perfoliatum*) has perfoliate leaves, connected at the base which clasps the stem.

FRUIT: Orange berries, about ⅓ inch in diameter, grow at the leaf axils; typically, three to five berries grow in each axil. Each berry has a small crown of narrow leaves, making the grouping of berries appear spiky. The fruit is inedible and will cause intestinal problems if eaten in large quantities, but the seeds of perfoliate horse gentian (sometimes called wild coffee) were roasted and used as a coffee substitute.

SEASON: Reddish-purple flowers (or yellow, in the case of yellow-flowered horse gentian) bloom in early summer, and are followed by elongated green berries, which enlarge and ripen in mid to late summer.

COMPARE: The alternating growth pattern of the leaves, and the flowers clustered in the leaf axils, make horse gentian easy to identify; once the berries develop, this plant can't be confused with any other.

NOTES: Horse gentian attracts bumblebees, which use their long tongues to extract nectar from the long-necked flowers.

green = key identification feature   * combined range

WOODY VINE

ALTERNATE LEAVES

LATE SUMMER TO FALL

American Bittersweet
Celastrus scandens

HABITAT: Found in rich woods, swamp edges, field edges, ravines and disturbed areas. Also grows on bluffs and rocky slopes. It grows best and produces more fruit in full sun, but will tolerate light shade.

GROWTH: A native perennial woody vine, bittersweet is often seen climbing on trees, fences and shrubs. It can grow to 30 feet in length. Bark of older stems becomes scaly and corky in appearance.

LEAVES: The glossy, dark green leaves have finely serrated edges and are roughly oval in shape with sharply pointed tips; they are 2 to 4 inches long and about one-half as wide. Leaves grow alternately on the vine, which has a slightly twisting habit, sometimes causing the leaves to appear to rotate along the stem. Leaves turn yellow and drop off in fall.

FRUIT: A round berry-like capsule, about ¼ inch across. Small clusters of fruits grow at the branch tips; fruits are green when young, ripening to yellowish-orange in late summer. In fall, the capsules split open to reveal seeds with a shiny, orange-red coating, which make an attractive fall display. The fruits are mildly toxic and should not be eaten.

SEASON: The vine flowers in late spring. Unripe fruits develop in early summer, maturing in late summer and splitting open in fall.

COMPARE: May be confused with Oriental bittersweet (*C. orbiculatus*), an aggressive introduced vine that kills other plants by smothering or girdling them. Young shoots of Oriental bittersweet have small thorns that are absent on American bittersweet; leaves of the Oriental variety tend to be wider, almost round. Oriental bittersweet fruits grow from the leaf axils rather than from the tips, and the insides of split-open capsules are yellow, while those of American bittersweet are orange.

NOTES: The fruits remain on the plants through winter, providing food for ruffed grouse, pheasant, quail, rabbit, songbirds and squirrels. Branches containing clusters of the dried, split-open fruits are used to add color to flower arrangements.

green = key identification feature

Oriental bittersweet

Split capsule of American bittersweet

LARGE
WOODY SHRUB

OPPOSITE
LEAVES

SUMMER
THROUGH FALL

• see below

Morrow's Honeysuckle –AND–
Tatarian Honeysuckle *Lonicera morrowii, L. tatarica*

HABITAT: Two types of non-native bush honeysuckle with orange berries inhabit our region: Morrow's (*Lonicera morrowii*, pictured at right), and Tatarian (*L. tatarica*, also pictured on pg. 150). Both are considered invasive due to their habit of crowding out native plants. They are extremely adaptable, and inhabit forest edges, waste ground, open woodlands, parklands and shelterbelts. They grow best in full sun with adequate moisture, but can tolerate shade and moderately dry soil conditions.

GROWTH: A large, multi-stemmed shrub, with spreading crown. Tatarian honeysuckle is up to 10 feet in height and width; Morrow's, up to 8 feet in height and width. Morrow's bark is light brown; young stems are slightly hairy. Bark of Tatarian honeysuckle is light gray; older branches often have shreddy bark that peels off in vertical strips.

LEAVES: Opposite, roughly oval, blue-green leaves, with short stemlets (petioles) and slightly rounded points on the tips; leaves are 1½ to 2½ inches in length. Morrow's leaves are slightly hairy underneath; Tatarian leaves are smooth on both surfaces.

FRUIT: A juicy, round orange or red berry, ¼ inch in size. Berries grow from leaf axils; they often grow in pairs, but each berry is distinctly round. Morrow's honeysuckle berries have a ½-inch-long stemlet; the berry stemlet is very short on Tatarian honeysuckle. Fruits of all non-native bush honeysuckle species are bitter and inedible.

SEASON: Bush honeysuckle are among the earliest plants to develop leaves in spring, and one of the last to lose their leaves in fall. Fruits are present from early summer through fall, and may persist over winter.

COMPARE: Please see the text on pg. 150 (bush honeysuckles with red berries) for information on similar-appearing plants.

NOTES: Birds devour honeysuckle berries, propagating the plants.

green = key identification feature   *combined range; specific IA locations not available

TREE

ALTERNATE
LEAVES

SUMMER

• see below

Peach

Prunus persica

HABITAT: According to the USDA PLANTS database, the domestic peach may be found occasionally in the wild in our area. American Indians cultivated peaches in Colonial days, taking seeds with them as they traveled. Wild trees may be survivors of those days, or remnants of gardens planted by farmers or homesteaders; they may also have grown from a picnicker's discarded peach pit. Peaches do best in well-drained, moist soil; they produce more fruit in sunny areas.

GROWTH: A small tree, up to 25 feet in height, with an open, rounded crown. Branches angle strongly upward, giving the plant a distinctive profile. Bark is gray and smooth, with prominent lenticels (breathing pores), becoming scaly and irregular as it matures; younger branches are smooth and reddish to greenish, with scattered pale lenticels.

LEAVES: A distinctly narrow leaf, 3 to 6 inches in length and one-third to one-quarter as wide; leaves often curve backwards, folding along the midrib. Edges are finely toothed; the top is shiny and dull green, the underside paler. Leaves grow alternately or in clusters on short petioles (stemlets).

FRUIT: An oblong to round drupe, generally 1 to 2 inches across, with a noticeable vertical cleft; the large stone is pitted. Ripe fruits are soft and juicy; the skin is fuzzy, and yellow with a reddish blush, although wild peaches may be lighter in color than domestic peaches. Flavor varies from tree to tree; some are very sweet, while others are tart or slightly bitter. All are edible; there are no toxic look-alikes. Peach leaves, twigs and seeds contain toxins, and should not be eaten.

SEASON: Peaches flower in early spring; fruits are ripe in midsummer.

COMPARE: Apricot (*P. armeniaca*) may rarely be found in the wild in scattered locations in Missouri and Illinois; its fuzzy golden fruits are smaller, and the leaves are wider, borne on long, reddish petioles.

NOTES: When sweet wild peaches are found, they are excellent eaten out-of-hand. Tart or slightly bitter peaches work well for pickling.

green = key identification feature   * specific IA locations not available

Apricot

TREE

ALTERNATE
COMPOUND
LEAVES

LATE SUMMER
THROUGH FALL

• see below

Mountain Ash

Sorbus decora, S. aucuparia

HABITAT: Two varieties of mountain ash inhabit our area: the native showy mountain ash (*Sorbus decora*), and the introduced European mountain ash (*S. aucuparia*). They are found on rocky ridges, in sun-dappled woods, and at the edges of forests. They require ample moisture and moderate to full sunlight; showy mountain ash is very cold-tolerant.

GROWTH: A small tree, generally no higher than 30 feet, with spreading branches and an open crown. Bark is smooth and brownish with numerous lenticels (breathing pores) when young, turning rough and gray with age.

LEAVES: Compound leaves with 11 to 17 leaflets grow alternately on the stems; leaflets are narrow with serrated edges, and paler below than above. Leaflets of showy mountain ash are about 2 inches long, with pointed tips; the overall leaf is up to 10 inches long. European mountain ash leaflets are 1 to 1½ inches long and coarsely serrated with blunt tips; overall leaf is 5 to 8 inches long.

FRUIT: Small pomes, each about ⅜ inch across, grow in dense clusters. Fruits are greenish-white when immature; European mountain ash ripens to bright orange, while showy mountain ash ripens to deep reddish-orange. It can be difficult to distinguish between species when confronted with them in the field; fortunately, fruits from both are edible. The fruit is somewhat astringent, becoming a bit milder after a frost. It is often used to make jelly, or as a seasoning for meat.

SEASON: Fruits ripen in late summer through fall, and remain on the trees through winter.

COMPARE: The native American mountain ash (*S. americana*) prefers colder climates, but may be found occasionally in the northern parts of our area; its leaves are similar to those of showy mountain ash but slightly narrower with a pointed base, and its fruits are bright orange.

NOTES: Mountain ash is an important fall and winter food source for birds including grouse, waxwings and grosbeak, as well as for black bears.

green = key identification feature   * combined range; specific IA locations not available

European mountain ash

TREE

ALTERNATE
LEAVES

LATE
FALL

Persimmon

Diospyros virginiana

HABITAT: Moist, well-drained areas including river bottoms, edges of streams, mixed-wood and hardwood forests. Persimmon tolerates damp soil and shade, but it produces more fruit in sunny areas.

GROWTH: This native tree can reach heights of 50 feet, although it is usually much shorter. Bark of a mature tree is dark gray, with raised, blocky patches, similar to flowering dogwood (pg. 184); the trunk often appears orangish between the raised areas. Twigs are light reddish-brown and hairy; they develop a zigzag habit as they mature.

LEAVES: Leaves are roughly oval, up to 6 inches in length and one-half as wide, broadest below the midpoint, with a softly pointed tip. They are deep green and smooth on top, paler underneath. They grow alternately on ½- to 1-inch-long downy petioles (stemlets). Edges are untoothed; the midvein is prominent, especially on the underside, and the leaves are slightly folded along the midvein.

FRUIT: A globe-shaped berry, generally 1 to 1½ inches across; the sepals (outer petals) remain on the fruit, forming a sturdy crown (like a thick strawberry cap), and there is a slender flower remnant on the base. The fruit has a whitish bloom; it has up to eight flat brown seeds, and a jam-like, sticky interior when ripe. When unripe, the fruit is extremely astringent, but when it ripens to deep orange and becomes soft and wrinkly, it is sweet and delicious. There are no toxic look-alikes.

SEASON: Flowers bloom in late spring; the fruit is green and hard most of the summer, ripening to deep orange in late fall, well after the leaves drop. It may remain on the trees through much of the winter. Some foragers wait to pick persimmons until they can be shaken from the tree or drop on their own, an indication of ripeness (Mike Krebill).

COMPARE: Persimmon leaves resemble those of blackgum (pg. 242), but blackgum produces small, oval drupes that are bluish when ripe.

NOTES: Persimmon wood is very dense, and is a favorite of woodworkers; it is also used to make pool cues and the heads of golf clubs.

green = key identification feature

Bark

Ripe fruit

Green persimmon

TENDER
LEAFY PLANT

OPPOSITE
LEAVES

LATE
SPRING

• see below

Lily of the Valley

Convallaria majalis

HABITAT: This common garden plant occasionally appears in the wild, and is found in areas with moist, rich soil, including dappled woodlands, disturbed ground, stream banks and roadsides. It prefers partial shade.

GROWTH: Each plant consists of two or three leaves growing from the same point from a green stem that arises straight out of the ground from the underground rhizome (root); the stem is 1 to 3 inches in length, and total plant height is 6 to 8 inches. White, fragrant, bell-shaped flowers grow in a staggered fashion from a thin stalk growing next to the stem; individual flower stemlets curve downward. The rhizomes spread easily; lily of the valley often forms dense colonies.

LEAVES: Lance-shaped leaves, with a tapered base and pointed tip, are typically 4 to 6 inches in length and about one-third as wide at the midpoint. Leaves have smooth edges, and fine parallel veins running from base to tip. They are smooth and bright green on both surfaces, and are sessile (attached directly to the stem).

FRUIT: Round red berries, about ¼ inch in diameter, grow in racemes (long clusters of multiple fruits). They are soft and juicy when ripe; each contains several small seeds. The berries contain toxic glycosides and should not be eaten.

SEASON: Flowers appear in early spring; fruits are ripe in late spring.

COMPARE: When it is not flowering, lily of the valley may be confused with ramps (*Allium tricoccum*; also called wild leeks), which have similar leaves; however, ramp leaves smell like onion when crushed, and ramp flowers grow in a rounded cluster at the top of the flowering stalk. In addition, ramps grow from a large white bulb, rather than from a rhizome; the bulb is a prime wild edible that is highly valued. The distinctions are important, because young ramp leaves are edible; lily of the valley leaves contain toxins and should not be eaten.

NOTES: Lily of the valley has been used as a medicinal plant.

green = key identification feature   * specific locations not available

TENDER
LEAFY PLANT

WHORLED
LEAVES

LATE SPRING
THROUGH
SUMMER

* see below

Strawberry

Fragaria virginiana, F. vesca

HABITAT: Prefers well-drained soil in full sun to part shade. Often found in rocky areas alongside rural roads, streams and lakes, and in open woodlands, disturbed areas, meadows and fields.

GROWTH: Two types of native wild strawberries inhabit our region: the Virginia or wild strawberry (*Fragaria virginiana*), and the less-common woodland strawberry (*F. vesca*). Both are erect, leafy plants 4 to 8 inches high, with white, 5-petaled flowers. Since both types spread by runners (horizontal stems), it's not uncommon to find a good-sized patch of wild strawberries.

LEAVES: Coarsely toothed trifoliate leaves grow at the ends of a long, fuzzy stem. The terminal tooth of a woodland strawberry leaf is longer than the surrounding teeth, while it is shorter than the surrounding teeth on a Virginia strawberry, helping distinguish the two varieties.

FRUIT: The heart-shaped strawberry is technically not a fruit; the actual fruits are the darker seeds embedded on the surface of the swollen receptacle (the base of the flower, which is normally inside the fruit). Woodland strawberries are about ½ inch long when mature; the seeds sit on the surface of the receptacle. Virginia strawberries are slightly smaller, and the seeds are slightly embedded in depressions on the surface of the receptacle. Both are rich red when ripe. Strawberries continue to flower throughout summer, so flowers and fruit are present at the same time once the season gets going.

SEASON: Strawberries flower from late spring through midsummer; tiny yellow fruits follow the flowers, swelling and ripening to a juicy red fruit a week or two later. Strawberries often produce fruit all summer.

COMPARE: Mock strawberries (pg. 110) have globe-shaped fruits with red seeds on the surface. Dewberries such as the dwarf raspberry (pg. 118) have similar trifoliate leaves, but the fruit is a compound drupe.

NOTES: Although smaller than commercial varieties, wild strawberries are sweeter and more intensely flavored, and well worth seeking.

green = key identification feature

* combined range

Virginia strawberry

Woodland strawberry

TENDER
LEAFY PLANT

ALTERNATE
COMPOUND
LEAVES

SUMMER

Red Baneberry

Actaea rubra

HABITAT: This native plant grows in shady areas of moist hardwoods and mixed forests. Often found in dappled woods alongside bracken fern and large-leafed aster.

GROWTH: Two to four doubly compound leaves, each up to 15 inches long, grow alternately on the main stem. The total height is 1 to 2½ feet. Flowers grow on a separate, leafless stalk that branches off one of the leaf stalks and generally rise above the surrounding leaves.

LEAVES: Three large compound leaflets grow on each of the long leaf stalks attached to the main stem; each has three or five smooth, sharply toothed leaflets oppositely attached by short stalks. The terminal leaflet is often slightly larger than side leaflets.

FRUIT: Firm, glossy berry about ⅜ inch long, slightly oval to round with a shallow vertical groove. Each berry has a small black dot at the bottom. Berries are typically red, although sometimes they are white. Berries grow in a cluster at the top of the thin flower stalk, and are attached to the stalk by thin, green stemlets. The berries are toxic.

SEASON: Ripe berries can be seen from early through late summer.

COMPARE: The related white baneberry (pg. 304) has similar leaves, but the flower stalk and stemlets are thick and knobby, usually reddish-pink, while those of the red baneberry are green and thin; the dot on the bottom of the berry is larger on white baneberries. Berry color is not always an accurate indicator of species, since red baneberry sometimes has white berries; the appearance of the flower stalk is a reliable indicator.

NOTES: All parts of the plant should be considered toxic; contact with leaves may cause skin irritation in sensitive individuals. Ingestion of the berries may lead to dizziness, vomiting or cardiac arrest; children are especially susceptible. Birds eat the berries with no ill effect, helping disperse the seeds.

green = key identification feature

Red baneberry
with white berries

TENDER
LEAFY PLANT

ALTERNATE
COMPOUND
LEAVES

SUMMER

Ground-Plum Milkvetch

Astragalus crassicarpus

HABITAT: This native perennial grows in open, rocky or gravelly areas, particularly those with limestone content. It is found in rocky meadows and prairie areas, along roadsides, and in sparse, rocky woodlands.

GROWTH: Stems grow from a central crown, and are typically 6 to 12 inches in length, although they may be longer. Stems are fleshy, and covered with fine hairs; they are reddish, or green tinged with red. Young stems are upright, but when fruits develop, the stems usually sprawl on the ground. In late spring, the plants have abundant clusters of pink to purple orchid-like flowers. Ground-plum have no tendrils.

LEAVES: Compound leaves, 2 to 5 inches in length, grow alternately. Leaves have seven to 16 pairs of small, narrow, lance-shaped leaflets on the hairy, pale-green leaf stemlet; a terminal leaflet is usually present. Leaflets are pale and dull green in color, with smooth edges; they average ¾ inch in length and are about one-quarter as wide Undersides are hairy; the top sides may be smooth, or have scattered fine hairs.

FRUIT: Plump, smooth-skinned, egg-shaped pods, about an inch long and containing numerous small black seeds, grow in clusters at the ends of non-leafy stems. Fruits are greenish when immature, ripening to brickish-red. They have two lengthwise seams; the bottom of the fruit bears a long, thin tail. *Immature* fruits are edible raw, cooked or pickled; care must be taken to ensure proper identification, as some plants with similar leaves and flowers have toxic fruits (see below).

SEASON: Fruits develop in late spring, ripening in early summer.

COMPARE: Other plants with similar leaves and flowers inhabit our area, but their fruits are shaped like pea pods, which may be flat or fattened in appearance; some are oval, like a large kidney bean. These include other *Astragalus*; purple locoweed (*Oxytropis lambertii*); and numerous vetches (*Vicia* spp.), which are vining plants with tendrils. Many of these pea pod-like or oval fruits are toxic; none should be eaten.

NOTES: Seek advice from a skilled forager before eating ground-plum.

green = key identification feature

• see below

TENDER
LEAFY PLANT

WHORLED
LEAVES

SUMMER

Trillium (several)

Trillium spp.

HABITAT: Four species of native trillium with reddish fruits inhabit our area: purple trillium (*Trillium erectum*), nodding trillium (*T. cernuum*), toadshade trillium (*T. sessile*) and bent trillium (*T. flexipes*). All four inhabit rich forests with ample moisture and moderate to heavy shade.

GROWTH: A single stem has a whorl of three broadly oval leaves at the top. The flower grows on a stalk that emanates from the center of the leaf whorl. After blooming, the sepals dry out but remain on the plant during fruit development. All four trillium species are generally about 12 inches in height, but can grow taller in good conditions.

LEAVES: Roughly oval, with smooth edges, deep veins and sharply pointed tips. Purple trillium leaves are 2 to 7 inches long and roughly as wide; nodding trillium, 2 to 6 inches long and slightly wider than long; toadshade, 2½ to 3½ inches long and half as wide; bent trillium, 4 to 10 inches long and roughly as wide. Toadshade leaves are green, mottled with silver; leaves of the other three are solid green.

FRUIT: Trillium have berry-like capsules with sharply defined edges; each has three internal chambers containing seeds surrounded by wet pulp. Fruit of purple and bent trillium sit above the leaves on a long stalk. Purple trillium fruit is ½ inch across and purplish-red; that of bent trillium is ¾ to 1½ inches across and pinkish-red. Toadshade trillium has dark greenish-purple fruit about ½ inch across that sits above the leaves, but there is no stalk. Fruit of nodding trillium is deep pink or red and about 1 inch across on a long stalk that curves down so the fruit is tucked under the leaves.

SEASON: Trillium flowers in the spring; fruits ripen in midsummer.

COMPARE: Four trillium species in our area have similar growth habits, but ripe fruits are greenish.

NOTES: Some trillium fruits are edible, while others are considered toxic. However, the plants are listed as endangered in many locations and fruits should not be disturbed.

green = key identification feature

*combined range

Nodding trillium

Purple trillium fruit

TENDER
LEAFY PLANT

ALTERNATE
LEAVES

SUMMER

Goldenseal

Hydrastis canadensis

HABITAT: This native plant is found in moist, shady deciduous woods, slopes, ravines and forest edges. Goldenseal prefers loamy soil that is rich with organic matter; it often is found in seasonally flooded areas.

GROWTH: A fuzzy stem grows from the yellowish rhizome (an underground root-bearing stem) to a height of 6 to 18 inches; a large palmately lobed leaf grows at the top of the stem. Some plants have a forked stem, with a leaf on top of each fork; only forked plants will flower and produce fruit. Goldenseal usually grows in large colonies.

LEAVES: The flowering/fruiting plant has two palmately lobed leaves. One leaf is usually larger, up to 9 inches in length, with almost equal width; a smaller leaf bears the fruit atop a short stemlet. Each leaf has three to seven lobes with toothy edges. Leaves are hairy on both surfaces, and are sometimes very wrinkly.

FRUIT: Ripe goldenseal fruit is a red, compound drupe about ½ inch across that somewhat resembles a red raspberry (pg. 130). Individual drupes of goldenseal are somewhat pointed, whereas the drupes of raspberries are rounded and more closely joined. The fruits are mildly toxic and should not be eaten.

SEASON: Fruit is green in late spring, ripening to red in summer.

COMPARE: Mayapple (pg. 64) has a similar growth habit, with a forked stem topped by a large leaf; however, the fruits bear no resemblance to one another. Red raspberries (pg. 130) somewhat resemble goldenseal fruit, but raspberries grow as an arching, thorny bramble.

NOTES: Goldenseal (particularly the rhizome) contains the alkaloids berberine, hydrastine and canadine, and has been used medicinally since pre-Colonial times. It has been used to treat everything from cancer, poor appetite, and diarrhea to fever, stomach problems, ringworm and earache. It has recently come into use as an augment for the immune system. Overharvesting and habitat loss have endangered native stocks of the plant, and it is now listed as an endangered species.

green = key identification feature

TENDER
LEAFY PLANT

WHORLED
LEAVES

MID TO
LATE SUMMER

Bunchberry

Cornus canadensis

HABITAT: This native plant inhabits cool, shady coniferous and mixed-wood forests; sometimes found in boggy or swampy areas.

GROWTH: Technically a shrub, bunchberry grows as a leafy plant that is typically 4 to 8 inches high. It grows from a spreading underground rhizome (root-bearing stem) and is often found in a large colony.

LEAVES: Each plant has one or two groupings of four to six leaves that grow oppositely; pairs grow so closely spaced on the stem that the leaf groups have a whorled appearance. The deep green, shiny leaves are oval, with pointed ends and deep veins that curve from base to tip; they are typically 1 to 3 inches in length, and about three-quarters as wide. A flower stalk rises from the center of the top leaf pair.

FRUIT: Round, bright red drupes, ¼ inch across, grow in a cluster from the flower stalk at the top of the plant. The fruits are edible, but mealy and bland with hard seeds, and are not worth seeking out. They can be eaten raw as a trail nibble, or cooked into jam, jelly, sauce or pudding. Bunchberry is a good survival food to know about.

SEASON: Tiny greenish flowers with large white bracts (leaves borne on a floral axis) appear from late spring through early summer; the flowers develop into fruits, which ripen in mid to late summer.

COMPARE: Canada mayflower (pg. 302) has leaves that somewhat resemble those of bunchberry, but Canada mayflower has only one to three leaves per plant, and its veins are much less pronounced. (A leaf of Canada mayflower is visible in the photo at right, just above the sliver of white wood to the right of the top bunchberry plant.)

NOTES: Bunchberries have a unique pollination method; when the closed flower is touched, it opens explosively—in less than a millisecond—to release its pollen, throwing it up to an inch away at a speed of 10 feet per second (according to a study reported in a 2005 edition of the journal *Nature*). Bunchberry is classified as endangered in Illinois, and threatened in Iowa.

green = key identification feature

TENDER
LEAFY PLANT

ALTERNATE
LEAVES

MID TO
LATE SUMMER

* see below

Asparagus

Asparagus officinalis

HABITAT: This escapee from cultivation is found in sunny pastures, fields, roadsides, and ditches, and along fencelines, embankments and railroad grades, especially those near agricultural areas.

GROWTH: Asparagus is a commonly grown vegetable that develops into a bushy, multi-stemmed fern-like plant with feathery, drooping fronds. It can grow up to 6 feet in height, with equal width. In mid to late summer, small red berries develop on the fronds.

LEAVES: The true leaves are actually small scales on the main stem; they are the same as the dark, dagger-like leaves on the stalk of the familiar asparagus shoot. The wispy, fern-like appearance of the plant comes from branches with soft, needle-like leaves; the branches grow alternately on the main stem.

FRUIT: Round red berries, about ¼ inch across or slightly larger, grow on thin, bent stemlets from the upper wispy branches. The berries are inedible.

SEASON: Asparagus shoots develop into the "asparagus fern" by early summer. Berries ripen to red by mid to late summer.

COMPARE: Asparagus is easy to identify at all stages. At a distance, the fern stage of the plant may resemble any number of overgrown leafy plants, but close inspection of an asparagus plant, with its scale-like leaves on the stalks, will confirm its identity. Check the base of the plant; you'll see the asparagus spears you're familiar with, but the pointy top has grown into the fern-like stems. You may even be able to see last year's withered, browned stalks (see small photo at right). Remember the location, and come back the following spring to harvest fresh, wild-grown asparagus spears.

NOTES: Wild asparagus is simply the cultivated vegetable that has escaped the farm or garden. Birds eat the red berries, and the wild plants are often found near farms that grow asparagus.

green = key identification feature   * specific MO locations not available

Closeup of base

Asparagus plant in "fern" stage

TENDER
LEAFY PLANT

OPPOSITE
COMPOUND
LEAVES

MID TO
LATE SUMMER

Jack-in-the-Pulpit

Arisaema triphyllum

HABITAT: Sun-dappled deciduous forests with adequate moisture.

GROWTH: An erect, native perennial, 1 to 3 feet in height, that grows from a thick tuber. Each plant has one or two compound leaves that grow at the top of long, thick stalks which are purplish-green. The flowering portion grows on a thick stalk from the base of the main stalk, and is quite distinctive. A tubular green sheath (called a spathe), with purple or white stripes, surrounds the clublike structure (called a spadix) that bears the actual flowers at its top; the spathe extends over the spadix at the top, forming a hood. The spathe can be up to 6 inches tall; the enclosed spadix is typically 2 to 3 inches in height.

LEAVES: A three-part leaf sits atop each long leaf stalk; leaflets are up to 6 inches long and broadly oval, with a sharply pointed tip. Leaflets are joined directly to the leaf stalk, with no petiole (stemlet). Leaves usually have died back or fallen over by the time the fruit is ripe.

FRUIT: An elongated, tightly joined cluster of shiny berries develops from the spadix; ripe berries are bright red. Individual berries are about ⅜ inch across; the cluster is 1 to 3 inches in height and about one-third as wide. The berries are mildly toxic and should not be eaten.

SEASON: Flowers are present in spring. Unripe green fruit is present much of the summer, ripening to bright red in mid to late summer.

COMPARE: The ripe red fruit cluster resembles that of several other plants, but the leaves help distinguish them. Green dragon (pg. 108) has a single leaf whose stem is wishbone-shaped, with multiple pointy oval leaflets. Red baneberry (pg. 94) has a loose cluster of red berries, and several doubly compound leaves; it looks lacy in comparison to Jack. American ginseng (pg. 112) has three or more five-part compound leaves.

NOTES: All parts of the plant contain calcium oxalate crystals, which cause an intense burning sensation if eaten.

green = key identification feature

Ripe fruit

TENDER
LEAFY PLANT

SINGLE
COMPOUND
LEAF

MID TO
LATE SUMMER

Green Dragon

Arisaema dracontium

HABITAT: This uncommon native plant is found in areas with rich, moist, well-drained soil such as dappled, rocky woodlands, ravines and at the bases of bluffs. It requires partial to fairly deep shade.

GROWTH: An erect perennial, 1 to 3 feet in height, that grows from a thick tuber. Each plant has a thick stalk (sometimes two), topped by a compound leaf having numerous unevenly sized leaflets. The flowering portion grows on a thick stalk from the base of the main stalk and is quite distinctive; its form gives the plant its common name. A tubular green sheath (called a spathe) surrounds the clublike structure (called a spadix) that bears the actual flowers. The top of the spadix, above the inconspicuous flowers, becomes thin and whip-like, extending several inches beyond the spathe; this is thought to resemble a dragon's tongue.

LEAVES: Each main stalk bears a single compound leaf, with a wishbone- or arc-shaped stem. The leaf stem joins the stalk at its center, often appearing to be two separate leaves that grow opposite one another at the top of the stalk. Each leaf has seven to 15 unequally sized oval leaflets, each with a pointed tip and tapered base; except for a few at the tip, leaflets grow to the outside of the stem.

FRUIT: An elongated, tightly joined cluster of shiny berries develops from the spadix; ripe berries are bright red. Individual berries are about ⅜ inch across; the cluster is 1 to 3 inches in height and about one-third as wide. The berries are mildly toxic and should not be eaten.

SEASON: Fruits ripen gradually, turning solid red in mid to late summer.

COMPARE: The ripe fruit is visually identical to that of Jack-in-the-pulpit (pg. 106), but the leaf structure is quite different; Jack's spathe is striped, and Jack does not develop the long, whip-like extension on the spadix. See the text on pg. 106 for additional look-alikes.

NOTES: All parts of the plant contain calcium oxalate crystals, which cause an intense burning sensation if eaten.

green = key identification feature

Ripening fruit

TENDER
LEAFY PLANT

ALTERNATE
COMPOUND
LEAVES

MID TO
LATE SUMMER

* see below

Mock Strawberry
–OR– **Indian Strawberry**

Duchesnea indica

HABITAT: Originally from Asia, mock strawberry is sometimes planted as an ornamental, and has escaped cultivation to become a pest in many areas. It is found in parks, lawns, open woodlands, fields and waste ground, growing best in partial shade.

GROWTH: A low-growing plant that creeps along in vine-like fashion. The trailing stem is hairy, and green to purplish-green; it roots at leaf nodes, often forming large, mat-like colonies. Individual stems may be a foot or more in length.

LEAVES: Three-part compound leaves grow alternately on long, hairy green petioles (stemlets). The oval leaflets have rounded teeth around the entire edge; they are up to 2½ inches in length and two-thirds as wide. Leaves have fine hairs on the top surface; underneath, the veins are also hairy.

FRUIT: A soft, fleshy red globe whose surface is covered with raised red seeds, the mock strawberry looks like a round, red-seeded version of the familiar strawberry. Mock strawberry grows upright on a hairy stem that arises from the leaf axils; green bracts (leaf-like structures) grow around the base of the fruit. The interior is pale pinkish-white. Although edible, mock strawberries are almost tasteless, and the faint flavor they do have is mildly unpleasant.

SEASON: Yellow flowers appear in profusion from late spring through midsummer; fruits are ripe from midsummer through late summer.

COMPARE: True strawberries (pg. 92) look similar, but the seeds on the surface are dark; leaves are toothed only on the top half, while the lower half of the leaf is smooth-edged. True strawberries have white or pale pink flowers.

NOTES: Some references list this plant as *Potentilla indica*.

green = key identification feature   * specific IA locations not available

Typical colony

TENDER
LEAFY PLANT

COMPOUND
LEAVES

LATE SUMMER
TO EARLY FALL

American Ginseng

Panax quinquefolius

HABITAT: Rich, moist hardwood forests and ravines; often found on north-facing slopes. Prefers shade, but will grow in dappled woods.

GROWTH: A smooth green stalk grows from the underground rhizome (root-bearing stem), with a whorl of compound leaves at the top. A separate, long flowering stalk rises from the joining point of the leaves. The total height of the plant is 12 to 18 inches.

LEAVES: Ginseng plants typically have three compound leaves, although there can be as many as five leaves per plant. Each leaf is on a long stalk. Leaves are typically five-parted and about 10 inches across; individual leaflets are roughly oval in shape, with a short stalk, pointed tips, toothy edges and a pronounced midvein. The length of individual leaflets ranges from 3 to 8 inches; frequently, the two leaflets closest to the center of the plant are much smaller than the others.

FRUIT: A cluster of shiny red berries grows on a long stalk from the center of the plant; berries are a flattened oval. The berries are inedible.

SEASON: Ginseng flowers in early to mid summer. Berries ripen in late summer to early fall.

COMPARE: The leaves of ginseng resemble those of Virginia creeper (pg. 222), but Virginia creeper is a vine, its berries are blue, and its leaf edges are more coarsely toothed. Sarsaparilla (pg. 244) has a cluster of compound leaves, but the fruiting stalk grows separately from the leaf stalk and is topped with black berries. The bright red berry cluster of ginseng may be mistaken for that of Jack-in-the-pulpit (pg. 106), but Jack has two compound leaves that are three-parted, the stems are thick and purplish, and the red fruit is an oblong cluster 1 to 3 inches tall on a thick stalk that grows from the juncture of the leaf stalks.

NOTES: Ginseng is highly valued for its rhizome, which has medicinal properties. Overharvesting of the wild plants has severely depleted native stocks; now, most ginseng is grown commercially and the wild plant is considered endangered in most of its range.

green = key identification feature

**TENDER
LEAFY PLANT**

**OPPOSITE
LEAVES**

**LATE SUMMER
THROUGH FALL**

Partridge Berry
–OR– Two-Eyed Berry

Mitchella repens

HABITAT: Deciduous and mixed-wood forests with rich, acidic soil; also found in bogs, along stream banks and in areas with sphagnum moss. The plant tolerates dry to moist soil.

GROWTH: A creeping, ground-hugging native plant that roots at the leaf nodes, spreading to form a low mat on the forest floor. It is typically 2 inches in height or less.

LEAVES: Rounded, glossy, deep green leaves, broad at the base and tapering to a rounded point, grow opposite one another on the long, trailing stem. Leaves are ½ to ¾ inch in length and slightly less wide; they are attached to the stem with short petioles (stemlets). The midrib is thick and noticeably lighter in color; edges of the leaves are smooth. The undersides are yellowish and lighter in color.

FRUIT: The smooth drupe, about ¼ inch across, has two small dimples or depressions, formed when the paired flower buds grow together. This gives rise to the common name "two-eyed berry." The fruit is red when ripe; there are no toxic look-alikes because the two "eyes" are very distinctive. The drupe is edible but not particularly tasty, and is not worth seeking out; it makes an acceptable trail nibble or survival food.

SEASON: Partridge berry produces white to pale pink flowers in early summer; the flowers are followed by the fruit, which ripens in late summer and may persist over winter if not eaten by birds.

COMPARE: Cranberry (*Vaccinium* spp.), bearberry (*Arctostaphylos uva-ursi*) and creeping wintergreen (*Gaultheria procumbens*) are small trailing plants like partridge berry, but leaves on these other plants are alternate, and fruits lack the two dimples. In our area, these three plants occur only rarely in northern Illinois; they are edible, so a mistake in identification would not be serious.

NOTES: Partridge berry is listed as threatened in Iowa.

green = key identification feature

CACTUS

LATE SUMMER
THROUGH FALL

* see below

Prickly Pear

Opuntia spp.

HABITAT: Prickly pear is a native cactus that is found in dry, sandy or rocky areas with ample sunlight; it is also found in glades, open pine forests, on prairies, and in scrubby areas. It can tolerate drought.

GROWTH: At least five species of *Opuntia* may be found in various parts of our area; all share similar characteristics. Their flat, thick pads are roughly paddle-shaped; they may stand upright, or may sprawl on the ground. Typically, pads are armed with very sharp thorns that grow in clusters. Thorn size and quantity varies with the different species, and some individual plants may have few or no thorns. A many-petaled flower grows from a fleshy green fruit that sits on top of the pad; most varieties have yellow flowers, but some are orange or red. Eventually, the flower falls off, and the fruit ripens to red or maroon.

LEAVES: Prickly pear have no true leaves; the thick pads grow singly or in clusters. They are generally 2 to 4 inches in length and half as wide.

FRUIT: Shaped like an elongated cup or a flat-topped egg, prickly pear fruit (called *tuna*) grows from the top edge of the pad, often in rows or clusters. A pale, cupped depression at the top shows where the flower was attached. Fruits are green when young, maturing to red or maroon; ripe fruits usually have a whitish bloom. Fruit size varies between species, and from plant to plant; they may be an inch long, or larger than a hen's egg. When ripe, the flesh is bright red, juicy and sweet, with many small, hard seeds. All prickly pear fruits are edible; there are no toxic look-alikes. *Caution: the fruits have fine, sharp bristles; handle with gloves, and singe over a flame before peeling.*

SEASON: Prickly pear generally flower in late spring through summer; fruits ripen in late summer through fall and may persist through winter.

COMPARE: When prickly pear are fruiting, they can't be confused with any other plant.

NOTES: The pads are edible when cooked, and have long been a staple food for American Indians; they are also used in Mexican cooking.

green = key identification feature

* combined range

Flower on top of fruit

WOODY
VINE

ALTERNATE
COMPOUND
LEAVES

SUMMER

Red Dewberry
–OR– **Dwarf Raspberry** *Rubus pubescens*

HABITAT: This native species prefers rich, moist areas, and is found in mixed or hardwood forests, swampy areas, damp thickets and low areas. It is often found in the same areas as the related black raspberry (pg. 258), sprawling beneath its taller kin. Red dewberry is considered threatened in Illinois.

GROWTH: Actually a weak-stemmed woody vine, dewberry is a low plant with erect leaves, found creeping along the ground; its vining habit is noticeable upon close inspection, and the vines often root at the tips. Stems are smooth or slightly hairy, with no thorns or bristles.

LEAVES: Coarsely toothed trifoliate leaves with a sharply pointed tip grow alternately on the trailing stem. Leaflets are smooth to somewhat hairy. The compound leaf is 2½ to 4 inches in length.

FRUIT: The compound drupe, ¼ to ½ inch across, resembles a red raspberry; however, the ripe fruit of the dewberry does not separate as easily from the receptacle (core) as the fruit of a ripe red raspberry does. Ripe dewberries are edible and sweet, although quality and taste varies from one plant to another.

SEASON: Dewberries in our area ripen in midsummer.

COMPARE: Several varieties of black dewberry grow in our area; see pgs. 260 and 272 for more information. Strawberry (pg. 92) has similar trifoliate leaves, but its fruit is not a compound drupe, and its leaflets have blunt tips. Red and black raspberries (pgs. 130, 258) have similar leaves, but grow as arching brambles several feet long. Goldenseal (pg. 100) has similar-looking fruits, but the leaves resemble large maple leaves; goldenseal fruits are mildly toxic.

NOTES: If you find red dewberries that are hard and dry, they may be unripe specimens of a variety that ripens to black. Let them ripen until soft, regardless of color, before harvesting.

green = key identification feature

WOODY
VINE

ALTERNATE
LEAVES

SUMMER
THROUGH FALL

• see below

Climbing Nightshade

Solanum dulcamara

HABITAT: Moist hardwood forests and thickets, swampy areas, waste ground, roadsides and streambanks. Climbing nightshade prefers partial shade and abundant moisture.

GROWTH: A sprawling, non-native vine that produces many slim, scraggly branches that climb over other plants. It can appear as a short plant, but often grows to 10 feet in length, occasionally even longer. Branches are green or purplish, and often hairy, when young, turning brownish-green, smooth and woody as they mature; the base of the plant is woody. Flowers are bright purple with yellow centers. All parts of the plant have an unpleasant smell when crushed.

LEAVES: Bright green, shiny, heart-shaped leaves grow alternately on the branches; many leaves have two ear-like lobes at the base. The petioles (stemlets) are slightly flattened. Overall leaf length is up to 3 inches; the ear-like lobes span a width of up to 2 inches.

FRUIT: The glossy, many-seeded berry is up to ½ inch long and usually slightly narrower, although it can also be round rather than egg-shaped. Berries are green when immature, turning orange and finally bright red when ripe. All parts of the plant, including the berries, are highly toxic.

SEASON: Berries are produced throughout summer and into fall, remaining on the plant even after the leaves have fallen off.

COMPARE: Eastern black nightshade (pg. 248) has similar fruits, but it has tiny white flowers and its berries are black when ripe; leaves lack the lobes at the base, and the plant is a tender perennial that is only 1 to 3 feet in height.

NOTES: This plant is also called woody nightshade or bittersweet nightshade, a reference to the bittersweet compound dulcamarine which is found in all parts of the plant, but especially the roots. It also contains solanine, a toxic alkaloid found in the green parts of the common Irish potato (*S. tuberosum*) and other members of the nightshade family.

green = key identification feature   *specific IA locations not available

WOODY
VINE

OPPOSITE
LEAVES

LATE SUMMER
THROUGH FALL

* see below

Honeysuckle (vining; several) *Lonicera reticulata* and others

HABITAT: Four varieties of native vining honeysuckle inhabit our region: grape (*Lonicera reticulata*, pictured at right), limber or twining (*L. dioica*), trumpet (*L. sempervirens*, which some sources consider a garden escapee) and yellow (*L. flava*). They are found in open forests and thickets, rocky areas, clearings, and along streams and ravines.

GROWTH: A climbing woody vine, 10 to 15 feet in length; it may bend down upon itself and appear shrublike. Stems of grape and yellow honeysuckle are finely grooved; trumpet and limber honeysuckle stems become shreddy with age. Trunks of all four have shreddy bark. Yellow, orange or red flowers grow in a cluster at the end of the vine.

LEAVES: Opposite, 1½ to 4 inches in length, attached directly to the stem or by a short petiole (stemlet). Grape honeysuckle leaves are widest, and may be almost round; the others are more oval. One or two pairs of leaves at the end of the stem are joined at the bases to form a cup. The cup of grape honeysuckle has a white bloom above; leaves may be slightly hairy below. Limber and yellow honeysuckle cups may have a slight bloom above. Leaf undersides are waxy, whitish and occasionally hairy on limber honeysuckle; undersides are smooth and pale but not bloomy on yellow honeysuckle. Trumpet honeysuckle leaves, including the cup, are semi glossy and smooth with no bloom.

FRUIT: Smooth, oval berries, ¼ to ⅜ inch long, grow on a stalk in a cluster from the center of the terminal leaf cup; berries have a bump on the bottom, and are reddish when ripe. They are very bitter and inedible.

SEASON: Flowers are present from late spring through midsummer. The berries ripen from late summer through early fall.

COMPARE: Japanese honeysuckle (pg. 256) is a non-native vine that is considered highly invasive; its black berries grow on stubby stalks from the leaf axils, and lack the joined leaf cup at the end of the stem.

NOTES: Yellow honeysuckle is not found in the wild in Iowa. It is considered endangered in Illinois.

green = key identification feature   * combined range; specific IA locations not available

WOODY
VINE

ALTERNATE
LEAVES

FALL

Carolina Coralbead
–OR– **Snailseed**

Cocculus carolinus

HABITAT: This native vine is found in areas with moderately rich, moist soil including thickets, bottomlands, glades, streambanks, forest edges, roadsides and open woodlands. It will tolerate partial shade to full sun.

GROWTH: A twining, woody vine that may grow to 12 feet long in our area; it will climb up fences, posts, telephone poles and other plants, or may recline on the ground. Young stems are thin, green and hairy; older stems are woody, with knobby, warty bark on the oldest parts. Coralbead has no tendrils; to climb, it winds itself around the supporting structure. It frequently has fairly dense foliage.

LEAVES: Heart-shaped to triangular leaves, 2 to 4½ inches in length and almost as wide, grow alternately on hairy petioles (stemlets) that are up to 4 inches in length. Leaves often have three to five rounded lobes; the central lobe is longest, and the overall outline of some leaves is said to resemble an elephant's head. Edges are smooth. Leaves are bright, deep green above, and are smooth or lightly hairy; undersides are paler and downy.

FRUIT: Bright red, glossy drupes, ¼ to ⅓ inch across, grow in hanging clusters from leaf axils; clusters may be up to 6 inches long. Each fruit has a single, flattened seed that is notched on one edge, with a deep dimple in the center; the edge looks like a textured coil, giving the plant its common name of snailseed. The fruits are bitter and inedible.

SEASON: Small, greenish flowers appear in summer; fruits ripen in fall.

COMPARE: The leaves and overall growth form of the plant resemble greenbrier and some other *Smilax* (pg. 250); however, greenbriers have prickles and thorns, which are absent on coralbead. Also, the *Smilax* in our area have fruits that are black when ripe.

NOTES: Coralbead leaves are eaten by deer and cattle; some birds relish the fruits.

green = key identification feature

Leaf resembles
an elephant's head

Snail-like seed

VINING
SUBSHRUB

OPPOSITE
LEAVES

LATE SUMMER
TO FALL

Running Strawberry-bush

Euonymus obovatus

HABITAT: This native plant is found in areas with rich, well-drained soil including thickets, woodlands and swamp edges. It prefers shade or dappled sunlight, and is often found on north-facing slopes (Don Kurz, *Shrubs and Woody Vines of Missouri*).

GROWTH: A ground-hugging, trailing plant, it is technically a subshrub, but vine-like in growth habit. Young stems are smooth and bright green, becoming purplish or brown with age; they are thin and flexible, and often develop roots where they contact the ground. Running strawberry-bush frequently grows in large, mat-like colonies; the plants are generally 12 inches or less in height, but individual stems can grow to several feet long as they sprawl on the ground.

LEAVES: Oval to egg-shaped leaves, broadest at or above the mid-point with a tapered base and roundly pointed tip, grow oppositely on short petioles (stemlets) that are sometimes grooved. Leaves are smooth and bright green, 1½ to 2½ inches in length and half to two-thirds as wide; edges have fine teeth. In fall, the leaves turn purplish or pink.

FRUIT: The most distinctive part of the plant. A warty-looking, rounded capsule, about ¾ inch across and slightly flattened, it grows on a thin stemlet from a leaf node. The capsule is white at first, turning pink or orange and eventually splitting into three parts to reveal two to four seeds with bright red, fleshy coating. The fruits are inedible.

SEASON: Fruit capsules develop from greenish flowers in early summer; the capsules are white in midsummer, turning pink and splitting open in late summer to early fall.

COMPARE: Bursting-heart (*E. americanus*) has similar fruits, but it is an upright shrub rather than a trailing plant; its leaves are broader toward the stem and the capsule is usually five-parted. In our area, bursting-heart is found only in scattered locations in the Missouri bootheel and in southern Illinois, where it is considered endangered.

NOTES: Fruits are eaten by wild birds; leaves are browsed by deer.

green = key identification feature

Ripe fruit

SMALL
WOODY SHRUB

ALTERNATE
COMPOUND
LEAVES

SUMMER

Fragrant Sumac
–OR– Skunkbush

Rhus aromatica

HABITAT: Relatively dry areas, including rocky slopes, glades, high stream banks, sand dunes and old pastures. Also found along rural roads and on waste ground. It prefers sun, but will tolerate light shade.

GROWTH: A spreading shrub that is generally 6 feet or less in height; may spread up to 10 feet in width. Twigs are smooth and brown, hairy when young but with no thorns or bristles; numerous branches usually rise above the mound of base foliage. *Rhus aromatica* is native to our area; however, hybrids are frequently planted in landscaping, and may be seen as non-native escapees in our area.

LEAVES: Glossy three-part leaves with scalloped edges grow alternately on long petioles (stemlets). Leaves are 4 to 6 inches long, dark green on top and lighter underneath. The end leaflet is joined directly to the two side leaflets by a long, tapering neck; it is generally larger than the side leaflets. When crushed, the leaves and stems have a noticeable scent which ranges, on individual plants, from pleasant to mildly skunky.

FRUIT: The distinctive hairy, red to reddish-orange drupes grow in clusters at the ends of the twigs. Individual drupes are about ¼ inch in length and slightly less wide. The drupes are lemony-sour and can be used to make a lemonade-type beverage. There are no toxic look-alikes.

SEASON: Fruits ripen in midsummer, and may persist through winter.

COMPARE: Poison ivy (pgs. 48 and 306) has three-part leaves that often have scalloped edges, but it has small ribbed berries that are greenish or white; also, the terminal leaflet of poison ivy has a long petiole.

NOTES: Although fragrant sumac is not a major wildlife food source, deer occasionally browse on the foliage and twigs; small mammals and birds eat the fruits, particularly in winter. The fruits were reportedly salted and eaten by pioneers. Some references list this plant as *R. trilobata*, a reference to the three-part leaves.

green = key identification feature

SMALL
WOODY SHRUB

ALTERNATE
COMPOUND
LEAVES

SUMMER

Red Raspberry

Rubus idaeus

HABITAT: Open woods, thickets, edges; one of the first plants to appear in an area that has been cleared or burned.

GROWTH: Red raspberries are brambles, sprawling vine-like shrubs that often form a thicket. Stems, called canes, grow to 5 feet in length, and are usually arching but may also be upright. Canes have round bristly stems but no thorns. Young canes are reddish or greenish in color; older canes are brownish and shreddy.

LEAVES: Compound, doubly toothed leaves with sharply pointed tips grow alternately on the canes; undersides are pale. Leaves usually have three to five leaflets, occasionally seven; they are up to 8 inches long. The terminal leaflet has a short petiole (stemlet), while the side leaflets are attached directly to the stem.

FRUIT: A compound drupe, up to ½ inch across and usually equal in length. Fruits are green and hard at first, turning pinkish and finally ripening to rich red. Ripe fruits detach cleanly from the plant, leaving the receptacle (core) behind; the picked fruit is hollow.

SEASON: Red raspberries ripen in midsummer, generally after black raspberries and well before blackberries.

COMPARE: Underripe black raspberries (pg. 258) resemble red raspberries, but canes have large thorns and a whitish bloom. Goldenseal (pg. 100) has similar-looking fruits, but leaves resemble large maple leaves; goldenseal fruits are mildly toxic and should not be eaten. Dewberries (pgs. 118 and 272) are low-growing plants with three-part compound leaves and smooth stems (except for bristly dewberry, pg. 260); the fruit does not detach easily from the receptacle. Thimbleberry and purple-flowering raspberry (pg. 132) have large maple-like leaves, and the fruit is wider. Blackberries (pg. 270) have similar fruits that are black when ripe; when red (underripe), they are hard and dry.

NOTES: Some red raspberry plants found in the wild are native plants, while others are descended from cultivated plants.

green = key identification feature

SMALL
WOODY SHRUB

ALTERNATE
LEAVES

SUMMER

• see below
Thimbleberry

Purple-flowering
raspberry

Thimbleberry –AND– Purple-Flowering Raspberry

Rubus parviflorus, R. odoratus

HABITAT: Openings in mixed-wood forests, along rural roads, edges and clearings. They produce more fruit in sunny areas with good moisture, but will tolerate light shade and somewhat dry soil.

GROWTH: Erect, leafy native shrubs that grow in large, open colonies. These two *Rubus* are very similar; they are best distinguished by the flower color, bud shape and size of the plant. Thimbleberry (*Rubus parviflorus*, main photo at right) has white flowers and is shorter, usually 3 feet in height or less; purple-flowering raspberry (*R. odoratus*) can grow to 6 feet in height. Older stems of both have shreddy or peeling bark; young stems are hairy or bristly, but have no thorns.

LEAVES: Large, light green leaves that resemble wrinkled maple leaves; 4 to 8 inches long and wide. Leaves have three to five pointed lobes, with coarsely toothy edges all around; they grow alternately on long petioles (stemlets). Undersides are paler and may be slightly hairy.

FRUIT: A compound drupe, ½ to ¾ inch across and fairly flat. Fruits are white and hard at first, turning pinkish and finally ripening to rich red; ripe fruits are very soft and juicy. Ripe fruits detach cleanly from the plant, leaving the receptacle (core) behind; the picked fruit is hollow, but so soft that it may crumble upon picking. Although seedy, ripe fruits are usually very delicious, with a slight acidic tang that balances the sweetness. Fruit quality varies from plant to plant.

SEASON: Fruits appear on the plants in early summer, and ripen in mid-summer; typically, they begin ripening at the height of the red raspberry season, and continue to ripen after the raspberries are finished.

COMPARE: Red raspberries (pg. 130) have similar-appearing fruits, but they grow as a prickly bramble with compound leaves; fruits are more rounded. Please see pg. 130 for information on other similar fruits.

NOTES: Purple-flowering raspberry is considered endangered in Illinois.

green = key identification feature   * specific IL locations not available

Thimbleberry

Purple-flowering raspberry

SMALL
WOODY SHRUB

ALTERNATE
LEAVES

MID TO LATE
SUMMER

* see below

Red Currant
Ribes rubrum, R. triste

HABITAT: Two varieties of red currant inhabit our region: the introduced garden red currant (*Ribes rubrum*, pictured at right) and the native swamp red currant (*R. triste*), which does not grow in Iowa. They inhabit cool, moist woodlands, swampy areas, clearings and streambanks.

GROWTH: A straggling shrub; swamp red currant is generally about 3 feet in height, while garden red currant can reach 5 feet in height. Stems are smooth; older branches are woody. Garden red currant tends to grow in an upright manner, while swamp red currant often sprawls along the ground. Currant shrubs have no thorns.

LEAVES: Attached alternately to the stem by a medium to long petiole (stemlet). Each leaf has three to five distinct lobes, resembling a maple leaf with rounded teeth. Leaves are 2 to 5 inches long; swamp red currant leaves are usually slightly hairy below, while those of garden red currant are usually smooth.

FRUIT: Round ¼- to ⅜-inch berries grow in racemes (long clusters of multiple fruits). Immature berries are green, turning red and somewhat translucent when ripe. Berries are smooth and glossy, and are tart but delicious when used in baking, or cooked into jelly, jam and other dishes. The red currants listed here are edible; there are no toxic look-alikes.

SEASON: Red currants ripen in mid to late summer.

COMPARE: Several shrubs with similar appearance and edible berries grow in our area. Black currants (pg. 266) are similar, but the berries are black when ripe. Gooseberries (pgs. 54, 136, 202 and 264) have similar leaves and growth habits, but all gooseberries have thorns at the leaf nodes. Gooseberry fruits grow in clusters of two or three, in contrast to currant fruits which grow in a raceme.

NOTES: If you find a currant with red berries, but the berries are hard and opaque, you may have found unripe black currants (pg. 266).

green = key identification feature   * combined range; specific locations not available

SMALL
WOODY SHRUB

ALTERNATE
LEAVES

MID TO LATE
SUMMER

Prickly –OR– **Pasture Gooseberry** *Ribes cynosbati*

HABITAT: Thickets and tangled areas, scrubby shelterbelts, and rich, moist woods, especially those along rivers or ponds.

GROWTH: A native arching shrub about 3 feet high. Mature stems may be smooth, but sometimes have scattered bristles; leaf nodes have one to three thorns that are ¼ to ⅜ inch long.

LEAVES: Attached alternately to the stem by a petiole (stemlet); each leaf node has one to three leaves. Each leaf has three to five distinct lobes, resembling a maple leaf with rounded teeth. Leaves are smooth on top, hairy underneath.

FRUIT: The ¼- to ½-inch round berry grows on a thin stemlet from leaf nodes, singly or in clusters of two or three. Berries have soft prickles, either overall or around the half of the fruit closest to the stem. Distinct stripes run longitudinally on the berry; a prominent flower remnant is present at the end of the berry. Prickly gooseberries are green when young, maturing to reddish-purple when ripe. Gooseberries are edible in both the green and ripe stages. There are no toxic look-alikes.

SEASON: Ripe fruits are present from mid to late summer.

COMPARE: Two other native gooseberries inhabit our region. Stems of smooth gooseberry (pg. 202) are finely hairy but not bristly; those of Missouri gooseberry (pg. 264) have scattered thin bristles. Fruits of smooth gooseberry are purplish-black when ripe, while those of Missouri gooseberry are black; neither has prickles on the berry. Currant shrubs (pgs. 134, 266) resemble gooseberry shrubs, but berries are typically borne in racemes (long clusters of multiple fruits).

NOTES: Ripe gooseberries are excellent in baked desserts, sauces and other dishes. Green gooseberries (pg. 54) are rich in pectin, and are used primarily for jam and jelly. Prickly gooseberries are not eaten raw; the prickles soften and become unnoticeable when the fruit is cooked.

green = key identification feature

SMALL
WOODY SHRUB

ALTERNATE
LEAVES

SUMMER
THROUGH FALL

Matrimony Vine –OR– Goji Berry *Lycium barbarum*

HABITAT: Also called wolfberry, this Asian native is grown as an ornamental, and has escaped into the wild. It is found on waste ground and disturbed sites, alongside roads and railroads, and in abandoned agricultural areas. It prefers sun, and requires moist, well-drained soil.

GROWTH: A somewhat straggly shrub with weak, thin branches; longer branches droop down, appearing vine-like. The stems are brownish, sometimes mottled with pale gray; thin lengthwise ridges are often present. Older bark is rough. Plants may have short thorns.

LEAVES: Lance-shaped, or sometimes oval with tapered ends. Leaves are up to 2½ inches in length and one-half to one-third as wide; the base tapers into a short, wide petiole (stemlet). Leaves grow alternately, sometimes in small clusters. Edges are smooth; the midrib is prominent. Both surfaces are smooth and dull green in color.

FRUIT: Oval berries, ¼ inch long and half as wide, grow on long stemlets from the leaf axils; the berry is joined to the stemlet with bell-shaped cap. The berries are reddish-orange when ripe, and contain numerous small seeds. Fully ripe berries are edible raw, juiced, cooked or dried. Underripe berries may contain toxins, and should not be consumed.

SEASON: Purple, bell-shaped flowers bloom from late spring through early fall; berries ripen throughout summer and into fall.

COMPARE: Chinese desert thorn (*L. chinese*) is a very similar plant whose leaves are more rounded. Barberry (pg. 144) has similar-appearing fruits, but its leaves are much smaller and the plant is always thorny. Climbing nightshade (pg. 120) is a woody vine with similar berries, but its leaves are broader and heart-shaped; nightshade berries are toxic.

NOTES: Goji is grown commercially in China; the berries are dried and sold for use in cooking. The juice is marketed as a health tonic, often with claims that it will increase longevity, fight cancer and arthritis, cure impotence and boost the immune system. The leaves are used to make tea, and shoots are cooked as a vegetable in Europe.

green = key identification feature

Thorns

SMALL
WOODY SHRUB

ALTERNATE
COMPOUND
LEAVES

LATE SUMMER
TO EARLY FALL

* see below

Rose Hip

Rosa spp.

HABITAT: At least 18 species of roses grow in the wild in our area; some are native, others are introduced. They grow in clearings, thickets and open forests; on waste ground; and along lakes, streams and rivers.

GROWTH: A bushy, multi-stemmed shrub, typically 1 to 4 feet in height, with equal spread; sometimes grows as a bramble (a vine-like shrub with arching branches). Stems are armed with thorns or prickles, which may be scattered or may blanket the stem thickly. Bark of larger stems is shiny and typically reddish-brown; smaller stems are green.

LEAVES: Compound leaves, each with three to eleven oval leaflets, grow alternately. Leaflets are bright green above, and typically have fine hairs on the underside; edges are sharply toothed. The compound leaf is typically between 2 to 4 inches long, usually slightly less wide.

FRUIT: The fruits, called hips, develop at the base of the flower; specific characteristics are quite variable. They range in shape from round to oval; ripe hips are typically red, but they are sometimes orange. Hips always have a group of withered sepals at the end of the fleshy swelling. All hips are edible, but they are filled with small, hard, bitter seeds and tiny, stiff, irritating hairs. The best hips for eating have a higher flesh-to-seed ratio. There are no toxic look-alikes.

SEASON: Roses bloom from late spring through summer; hips develop afterwards, and are hard and green most of the summer, ripening in late summer to early fall. They typically persist through winter, and become softer and sweeter after a frost.

COMPARE: Roses are easy to identify, especially when hips are present; no other plant compares to a rose.

NOTES: Rose hips are rich in nutrients, particularly vitamin C. They may be eaten raw or cooked; palatability varies between species, so try a few from the plants you've found before collecting too many. Rose hips are often dried and brewed for tea. Cooked rose hip purée is similar to applesauce, and can also be used in baked goods.

green = key identification feature

* combined range

SMALL
WOODY SHRUB

ALTERNATE
LEAVES

LATE SUMMER
TO EARLY FALL

• see below

Canada Yew

Taxus canadensis

HABITAT: Shady, cool sites in coniferous or mixed-wood forests. Also found along stream banks, edges of bogs and swamps, and other moist, shady areas. Found in old-growth forests, rather than new growth.

GROWTH: A native, bushy evergreen shrub, up to 5 feet in height but usually shorter. Branches grow thickly in an upright spray. The bark of larger stems is reddish; older stems may have large, grayish scales. Yew plants are unisexual—a plant is either male or female, and each produces a different type of flower. Only female plants bear fruit.

LEAVES: Flat, dark green evergreen leaves with sharp tips grow thickly on soft twigs. The leaves are attached alternately in a spiral pattern; they are bent at the bases so they appear to grow in a flat plane from the twig. Leaves are up to 1 inch in length, and less than ⅛ inch wide.

FRUIT: A soft, bright reddish-orange cup called an aril surrounds a single seed; the aril is about ½ inch wide. Yew arils can be eaten by humans, but the seed and all other parts of the plant are dangerously toxic. It's not worth taking the risk; leave the aril alone, and let the birds eat the seeds (birds won't be harmed by eating them).

SEASON: Fruits are green, hard and small in midsummer, swelling and ripening in late summer through early fall.

COMPARE: There are no species in the wild in our region which could be confused with Canada yew. A cultivated yew species, Japanese yew (*T. cuspidata*), looks similar, but its leaves are broader; it occurs in the wild occasionally in the northeastern portion of the United States.

NOTES: All parts of yew except the aril (seed cup) contain taxanes, highly poisonous alkaloids which are toxic to humans and most animals. Deer, however, are not affected by the alkaloids, and browse extensively on the leaves; in some areas, yew have become scarce due to deer depredation. Birds eat the seeds contained in the aril, but are not harmed because the seeds pass through before the protective seed coat is dissolved.

green = key identification feature   * specific IA locations not available

SMALL
WOODY SHRUB

ALTERNATE
LEAVES

LATE SUMMER
TO EARLY FALL

• see below

Japanese Barberry
Berberis thunbergii

HABITAT: This is a cultivated plant that has escaped into the wild; it is drought-tolerant, and highly adaptable. It is often found on the fringes of urban areas, in both moist and dry areas. Also grows in open hardwood or mixed-wood forests, pastures, disturbed areas and meadows.

GROWTH: A dense, rounded shrub with arching branches that often extend beyond the mass of the shrub; 3 to 6 feet in height and slightly wider. Leaf nodes have a sharp thorn, about ½ inch long. The thin, reddish stems are grooved, and zigzag slightly at leaf nodes.

LEAVES: Paddle-shaped, broadest near the tip with a tapering base; deep green, with smooth edges and a deeply cleft midvein. Leaves are ½ to 1 inch long, and about one-half as wide, and grow in clusters of two to six; the clusters alternate along the stem.

FRUIT: Oblong, shiny berries grow on a long stalk from the leaf nodes; the berries are usually abundant. Berries are up to ½ inch in length, and sometimes so narrow that they appear cylindrical. They are yellowish when immature, ripening to opaque scarlet. The berries are dry, with a sharp, sour flavor; they are dried and used in Mideastern cooking.

SEASON: Berries ripen in late summer to early fall. The red berries often remain on the plant through winter, after the leaves have dropped.

COMPARE: European barberry (*B. vulgaris*) has a similar growth habit, and may be encountered in our region as a garden escapee; however, the berries grow in racemes (long clusters), and its leaf edges are toothy. American barberry (*B. canadensis*) is a native barberry that is very rarely seen in our area, and is considered endangered in Illinois; its leaves have 5 to 9 bristle-tipped teeth.

NOTES: Japanese barberry was introduced as an ornamental in the late 1800s; it has escaped cultivation and often crowds out native plants. It also alters soil chemistry by raising the pH level; this often causes native plants to suffer. Birds consume the prolific berries, spreading the plant; it is considered invasive in most areas in which it appears.

green = key identification feature   * specific IA locations not available

Thorns and unripe fruit

Ripe fruit

SMALL
WOODY SHRUB

OPPOSITE
LEAVES

FALL

Coralberry –OR– Buckbrush *Symphoricarpos orbiculatus*

HABITAT: This native shrub grows in dry, sunny areas including pastures, abandoned agricultural fields, rocky bluffs, glades, thickets and open woods; often found alongside roads and railroads.

GROWTH: An open, twiggy, multi-stemmed shrub, up to 4 feet in height but often shorter; it spreads by rhizomes (root-bearing stems) and often forms large colonies. Branches are thin and flexible, often arching downward, especially when bearing fruit. Young stems are tan to purplish and downy, later becoming smooth and brown. The trunk has flaky or shreddy brown bark.

LEAVES: Egg-shaped, with a rounded or tapered base and roundly pointed tip; 1½ to 2 inches in length and two-thirds as wide, broadest at or below the midpoint. Leaves grow oppositely on very short petioles (stemlets); the edges are untoothed, and may have fine hairs (visible with a lens). The top surface is bluish-green and smooth; undersides are paler and typically hairy, with pronounced veins.

FRUIT: Tight, sometimes blocky clusters of round to egg-shaped drupes, each about ¼ inch long, grow at leaf axils and at the tips of the branches; a crown-like floral remnant is present on the base. The fruits are opaque, rosy reddish-purple when ripe. They are not edible.

SEASON: Tiny, greenish flowers appear underneath the leaves at the leaf axils in midsummer; fruits develop slowly, ripening in fall. The fruits may persist over winter unless eaten by wildlife.

COMPARE: Bush honeysuckles (pgs. 82 and 150) have numerous berries along the stem, but they are bright red or orange, and translucent. Coralberry also may be mistaken for a young border privet (pg. 284), but privet's leaves are thick and leathery; ripe fruits are black. Bush honeysuckles and privet are much larger than coralberry when mature.

NOTES: The leaves and twigs are browsed by deer and other mammals; birds sometimes nest in the dense growth, and some eat the berries, although they do not appear to be a favored food.

green = key identification feature

LARGE
WOODY SHRUB

OPPOSITE
COMPOUND
LEAVES

EARLY TO MID
SUMMER

Red Elderberry

Sambucus racemosa

HABITAT: Common along habitat edges: roadsides, forest borders, shorelines and fence rows. Requires cool habitat; in the southern part of our area, it inhabits moist areas with dappled shade, and is often found on north- to northeast-facing slopes (Don Kurz, *Shrubs and Woody Vines of Missouri*).

GROWTH: A large, fast-growing native shrub, sometimes appearing as a small tree. Up to 20 feet in height, but also found much shorter. Bark of older stems is gray to reddish-brown, and covered with numerous warty lenticels (breathing pores). Younger stems are soft and pithy, and often covered with downy hairs.

LEAVES: Compound leaves, each with five to seven leaflets, grow oppositely on the stem; leaves are 6 to 10 inches long and nearly as wide. Leaflets are 2 to 5 inches long and one-third as wide, oval with a rounded base and pointed tip; edges are sharply toothed. Top sides are dark green and smooth, undersides are paler and may be downy.

FRUIT: Round drupes, about ⅛ inch across, with two seeds, grow profusely in upright, rounded clusters atop stalks that rise from the leaf axils; fruits are bright red when ripe. The fruits are rank in flavor and somewhat toxic, especially when raw; cooking may render the fruit—but not the seeds—edible, but opinions vary. Leaves, stems and all other parts of all elderberry species are toxic.

SEASON: Berries ripen in early to mid summer, well before those of the common elderberry (see below).

COMPARE: Common elderberry (pg. 204) has similar growth habits, but ripe fruits are purplish-black, and grow in flat-topped clusters rather than the rounded clusters of red elderberry; common elderberry leaves have five to 11 leaflets. Fruits of common elderberry are edible when cooked.

NOTES: Red elderberry is one of the first shrubs to flower in the spring. The fruits are eaten by many species of birds.

green = key identification feature

LARGE
WOODY SHRUB

OPPOSITE
LEAVES

SUMMER
THROUGH FALL

• see below

Bush Honeysuckle (several)   *Lonicera* spp.

HABITAT: Five types of non-native bush honeysuckle with red berries inhabit our region: Morrow's (*Lonicera morrowii*, pictured on pg. 82), Amur (*L. maackii*, pictured at right), Tatarian (*L. tatarica*, pictured at right), European fly (*L. xylosteum*) and showy bush honeysuckle (*L. × bella*). All are considered invasive. They are highly adaptable, and inhabit forest edges, parklands and shelterbelts. They prefer full sun with ample moisture, but tolerate shade and moderately dry soil.

GROWTH: A large, multi-stemmed shrub, with spreading crown. Amur honeysuckle is the largest, up to 15 feet in height with equal spread. Tatarian honeysuckle is up to 10 feet in height and width; European fly, 8 to 10 feet in height and width; Morrow's and showy bush honeysuckle, up to 8 feet in height and width. Bark on older branches is often shreddy, peeling off in vertical strips.

LEAVES: Opposite, oval leaves, 1 to 2½ inches long, with short petioles (stemlets). Amur leaves are shiny and dark green, with a sharply pointed tip. Morrow's and showy bush honeysuckle are blue-green and slightly hairy underneath; tips are rounded. Tatarian honeysuckle's leaves are blue-green and smooth, with a tip that is pointed but not as sharp as Amur's. European fly are grayish-green and hairy.

FRUIT: A juicy, round red berry, ¼ inch in size; berries of Morrow's and Tatarian may be orange when ripe. Berries often grow in pairs and may appear to be joined at the base, but each berry is distinctly round. The berries are bitter and inedible.

SEASON: Berries are present from summer through fall.

COMPARE: Canada fly honeysuckle (*L. canadensis*), found in our area only occasionally in northern Iowa and Illinois, is a native honeysuckle that is shorter, typically 3 to 5 feet; its red paired fruits are joined at the base and pointed at the tips. Please also see the text about orange-berried honeysuckles (pg. 82) for more information.

NOTES: Birds devour honeysuckle berries, propagating the plants.

green = key identification feature   * combined range; specific locations not available

Amur honeysuckle

Tatarian honeysuckle

LARGE
WOODY SHRUB

ALTERNATE
COMPOUND
LEAVES

MID TO
LATE SUMMER

Prickly Ash
–OR– Toothache Tree

Zanthoxylum americanum

HABITAT: Moist, sun-dappled hardwood and mixed-wood forests; river bottoms, ravines and thickets; bluffs and rocky hillsides.

GROWTH: A thorny, multi-stemmed native shrub, typically 8 to 10 feet in height; occasionally up to 25 feet high. Bark is brown or gray; twigs are reddish-brown with white spots. Bark sometimes splits, revealing yellowish wood. Stems are armed with thorns that are up to ½ inch long. All parts of the plant have a citrus fragrance.

LEAVES: Compound leaves, up to 10 inches long, with five to 11 leaflets, grow alternately. Leaflets are oval, ¾ to 3 inches long and one-half as wide, with broad bases and softly rounded tips; dull green above, paler below. The terminal leaflet is on a short petiole (stemlet); all others attach directly to the greenish stem.

FRUIT: Rounded, berry-like fruits grow in clusters along the stems. Fruits are reddish to orangish at maturity, and have a bumpy texture. They are technically follicles, dry capsules containing seeds; they split open when ripe to release the shiny black seeds. The fruits are inedible, but in the past they were reportedly chewed to relieve toothache. According to *The Dictionary of Useful Plants* (Nelson Coon; Rodale Press), the seeds may be cooked and used as a pepper substitute.

SEASON: Fruits ripen in mid to late summer, splitting open to release their seeds (one or two per follicle) by summer's end.

COMPARE: There are no confusing look-alikes. Leaves resemble those of the locust family (*Robinia* spp.) but locusts bear fruits that are flat and pod-like. The unusual fruits of prickly ash make this plant unmistakable when it is bearing fruit.

NOTES: The flowers, which are inconspicuous and appear in spring, attract bees. Wildlife, including vireo and other birds, rabbits and chipmunks, eat the fruit; giant swallowtail butterfly larvae eat the leaves.

green = key identification feature

LARGE
WOODY SHRUB

ALTERNATE
LEAVES

LATE
SUMMER

Common Chokecherry

Prunus virginiana

HABITAT: Mixed-woods or hardwood forests, clearings, parklands, slopes, river and creek embankments. In the northern part of our area, choke-cherries thrive in full sun; in the southern part, they require moist areas with partial shade.

GROWTH: A large native shrub, up to 25 feet in height but usually much shorter. Generally open in form and somewhat straggly. Bark is reddish-brown to gray and is smooth, with visible lenticels (breathing pores); smaller stems are often reddish. Shrubs frequently form thickets.

LEAVES: Broadly oval, smooth leaves grow alternately on petioles (stem-lets) that are often reddish. Leaves are dark green above, paler underneath; edges are finely toothed. Leaves are 2 to 4 inches long, roughly one-half as wide, tapering at or beyond the middle of the leaf to a broad point. The petiole has several small glands (visible with a lens).

FRUIT: Shiny round drupes, ⅜ inch across, grow in racemes (long clusters of multiple fruits). Ripe fruits are bright red to reddish-purple; they are soft and somewhat translucent. Each drupe contains a single egg-shaped pit which is fairly large in proportion to the amount of flesh. Chokecherries have a delicious sweet-tart flavor, although they are quite astringent when eaten raw. There are no toxic look-alikes.

SEASON: Chokecherries ripen in late summer.

COMPARE: Black cherries (pg. 296) have similar long clusters of fruits, but the leaves are much narrower and have reddish hairs along the midrib on the underside. Pin cherries (pg. 178) have narrower leaves; fruits are bright red when ripe and grow in small clusters, each on its own stem, rather than in racemes. Serviceberries (pg. 208) have similar leaves, but the fruit is a pome, an apple-like fruit with a crown.

NOTES: Chokecherry leaves and pits contain hydrocyanic acid, a cyanide-producing compound. The leaves and pits should never be eaten, and care should be taken to avoid crushing chokecherry pits when juicing the fruits. Cooking, drying or freezing eliminates the acid.

green = key identification feature

Chokecherry bark

EDIBLE

LARGE
WOODY SHRUB

OPPOSITE
LEAVES

LATE SUMMER
TO EARLY FALL

Guelder rose

Highbush
cranberry

Guelder Rose
–AND– Highbush Cranberry *Viburnum opulus, V. trilobum*

HABITAT: Moist, sun-dappled mixed-wood forests and thickets; swampy areas; river valleys and stream banks; edges and clearings.

GROWTH: These two similar-looking plants are multi-stemmed shrubs with rounded crowns, up to 15 feet high and wide. Bark is smooth and grayish-brown. Guelder rose (*Viburnum opulus*), also called European cranberry, is an introduced species that has naturalized in many areas. Highbush cranberry (*V. trilobum*) is a native plant.

LEAVES: Three-lobed leaves with well-defined veins resemble maple leaves; they attach oppositely to the stems on grooved petioles (stemlets). Leaves of guelder rose are typically 2 to 4 inches in length and width; those of highbush cranberry are up to 5 inches in length and slightly less wide. Lobes on both are sharply pointed, with numerous irregular teeth on each lobe; highbush cranberry is less toothy. Tiny glands at the base of the leaf stalk, visible with a lens, are concave on the guelder rose, and convex or dome-shaped on highbush cranberry.

FRUIT: Bright, shiny, red drupes grow in large, showy clusters. Individual drupes are ¼ to ½ inch long and slightly narrower. Fruit clusters grow on a long, reddish stem, and may droop with the weight of the fruit. Ripe, soft fruits of highbush cranberry are tart but edible, with a taste similar to commercial cranberries; they are used to make jelly, jam or sauce. Guelder rose fruits are very bitter; although edible, they are seldom gathered by foragers. There are no toxic look-alikes.

SEASON: Fruits ripen in late summer to early fall, and may persist on the plant through winter.

COMPARE: Maple-leaf viburnum (*V. acerifolium*) is similar, but ripe fruits are dark blue; in our area, it is found only in northern Illinois.

NOTES: Highbush cranberries aren't related to true cranberries (*Vaccinium* spp.), but they taste similar, giving them their common name.

green = key identification feature

Guelder rose

Highbush cranberry

LARGE
WOODY SHRUB

ALTERNATE
LEAVES

LATE SUMMER
TO EARLY FALL

Possumhaw

• see below
Winterberry

Possumhaw
–AND– Winterberry

Ilex decidua, I. verticillata

HABITAT: These native shrubs grow in moist to wet locations including damp mixed-wood forests, thickets, pond and stream edges, and swampy and boggy areas. Plants in full sun produce more fruits.

GROWTH: Both are erect shrubs with many branches. Possumhaw may be 25 feet in height, although it is usually shorter; winterberry is 20 feet or shorter. Both produce suckers (shoots), and are often found in large clumps. Bark on mature stems is dark gray to brown, smooth, and mottled with lighter spots. Winterberry twigs are purplish-brown, while those of possumhaw are light gray; both have scattered lenticels (breathing pores). These plants are generally unisexual—a plant is either male or female, and each produces a different type of flower.

LEAVES: Elliptical leaves that taper at both ends are attached alternately to the stems on short petioles (stemlets). Possumhaw leaves are 2 to 3 inches long and one-half as wide, with rounded teeth. Winterberry's leaves are up to 4 inches long and one-third as wide; edges have small, sharp teeth, especially on the top two-thirds. Leaves of both are glossy and bluish-green with a fine network of veins; undersides are paler and downy.

FRUIT: Smooth, glossy, opaque bright red berries, ¼ inch across with short stemlets, grow profusely in clusters from the leaf axils of female plants. The berries are inedible, and may cause intestinal problems.

SEASON: Berries ripen from late summer to early fall, and may persist through midwinter, making a striking display.

COMPARE: American holly (*I. opaca*) has similar berries, but leaf edges have very sharp, long teeth. Please also see pg. 168 for information on other shrubs with multiple red berries along the branches.

NOTES: "Possumhaw" is also used to refer to an unrelated species, *Viburnum nudum*, which somewhat resembles nannyberry (pg. 292).

green = key identification feature   * specific IA locations not available; listed as endangered

Possumhaw

Winterberry

LARGE
WOODY SHRUB

ALTERNATE
LEAVES

LATE SUMMER
TO EARLY FALL

• see below

Autumn Olive

Elaeagnus umbellata

HABITAT: Open woodlands, grassy areas, waste ground, roadsides and fencerows. Grows in a variety of soils, from sandy, loamy soil to fairly heavy clay soil with good drainage. The roots fix nitrogen, allowing it to thrive in poor soils. Does best in full sun, but tolerates light shade.

GROWTH: A large non-native shrub, up to 15 feet tall with equal width. Somewhat straggly, often considered weedy-looking; tends to form thickets. The entire plant has a silvery appearance. Stems are silver-brown, with brown scales. Branches may have scattered small thorns.

LEAVES: Silvery-green leaves grow alternately on short, scaly petioles (stemlets). Leaves are elliptic, 2 to 4 inches long and one-half as wide, tapering at both ends. Undersides are silvery and often have brown dots, especially early in the season. Edges are wavy but untoothed.

FRUIT: Oval to round drupes, ⅓ inch long, are covered with silver scales; fruits are plump and red when ripe. Quality varies from plant to plant. The best fruits are juicy and delicious; others have an astringent aftertaste. Choice fruits can be pulped or juiced. There are no toxic look-alikes.

SEASON: Fruits are hard, brownish and scaly in early summer; as the season progresses, they turn yellow with brown dots, finally ripening to a juicy red at the end of summer or in early fall.

COMPARE: Russian olive (pg. 76) has a similar silvery appearance, but its leaves are much narrower; ripe fruits are oblong, yellowish and dry. Russet buffaloberry (*Shepherdia canadensis*) has similar scales on the fruit, twigs and leaves, but its leaves are opposite and much shorter; in our area, it is found only rarely in northeastern Illinois, where it is considered endangered. Silver buffaloberry (*S. argentea*) is also similar in appearance, but the stems are thorny; it is a western plant, found in our area only in western Iowa, where it is listed as threatened.

NOTES: Autumn olive was widely planted during the 1800s; it is considered invasive because it shades out native understory plants.

green = key identification feature   * specific locations not available

Underside of leaf

LARGE
WOODY SHRUB

ALTERNATE
LEAVES

LATE SUMMER
TO EARLY FALL

Northern Spicebush

Lindera benzoin

HABITAT: Rich, moist deciduous woodlands and streambanks. Also found in ravines, valleys and bottomlands. Prefers full sun to partial shade.

GROWTH: A rounded, open native shrub, 8 to 12 feet in height, with equal spread. All parts of the plant have a spicy scent, especially when bruised. The bark is dark brown, and has numerous small, raised, light-colored bumps scattered along the main stem and older twigs. Spicebush plants are unisexual—a plant is either male or female, and each produces a different type of flower.

LEAVES: Smooth, glossy leaves are oval, tapering on both ends; 2 to 5 inches long, roughly one-half as wide, widest at the midpoint or slightly towards the tip. Edges are smooth; the tip has a sharp point. Leaves are medium green above, lighter below, and grow alternately on the stems on a short petiole (stemlet); veins are prominent on both surfaces. The alternating stems often have several leaves, of widely varying sizes, clustered together.

FRUIT: Shiny oval drupes, about ½ inch long, grow on short stemlets in small clusters along the branches of the female plants; fruits are red when ripe. The base has a small indentation. The fruit is used as a seasoning; it has a spicy, fruity flavor similar to allspice. There are no toxic look-alikes that have the spicy scent of spicebush.

SEASON: Fruits are present on the plant starting in midsummer. They are greenish when immature, ripening in late summer to early fall.

COMPARE: Southern spicebush (*L. melissifolia*) is a related species that appears in our area only rarely in Missouri; fruits are larger and the leaves are narrower. It is listed as endangered throughout the US.

NOTES: The leaves and twigs can be used to brew a spicy tea. White-tailed deer browse on the plants, as do other woodland mammals including cottontails and opossums. Songbirds, and upland birds such as quail and pheasants, feed on the fruits. The plant is host to the larval stage of the spicebush swallowtail butterfly.

green = key identification feature

LARGE
WOODY SHRUB

OPPOSITE
LEAVES

LATE SUMMER
TO EARLY FALL

Buttonbush

Cephalanthus occidentalis

HABITAT: Swampy and marshy areas; seasonally flooded ground; also along edges of ponds, lakes, rivers and streams. Buttonbush can't survive dry conditions or drought; it does best in full sun.

GROWTH: An open, straggly native shrub, generally 6 to 10 feet in height with equal spread; in favorable conditions, it may be taller. It often grows in dense colonies. Young stems are reddish-brown; older bark is grayish-brown and flaky. The distinctive flowering head is a 1-inch ball with numerous, tiny white flowers with thin, protruding stalk-like styles (the part of the flower that has the pollen-collecting part on its tip); the overall effect is that of a flowery pincushion stuck with many pins.

LEAVES: Glossy, smooth, bright green leaves grow oppositely on thin petioles (stemlets); some also grow in small whorls. Leaves are 3 to 5 inches long and one-third to one-half as wide; they are roughly oval, with a tapered base and a sharply pointed tip. Leaf edges are smooth; the midrib and veins are prominent.

FRUIT: A dull red ball, about ¾ inch across, with **numerous blunt nutlets** that give the ball a **nubby appearance.** The fruiting ball often persists through the winter. The fruits and leaves are toxic.

SEASON: Buttonbush flowers in the middle of the summer; the fruits replace the flowers in late summer, and are green at first, ripening to dull red in late summer to early fall.

COMPARE: When buttonbush has flowers or fruit on it, it is unmistakable and can be confused with no other plant.

NOTES: American Indian peoples in the southern United States used a tonic made from buttonbush bark to treat intestinal problems. Many kinds of moths and butterflies are attracted to buttonbush flowers; waterfowl eat the fruits.

green = key identification feature

LARGE
WOODY SHRUB

OPPOSITE
LEAVES

LATE SUMMER
TO FALL

* see below

Winged Euonymus

Euonymus alatus

HABITAT: This fast-growing Asian native has been widely planted as an ornamental, and has escaped cultivation to become a nuisance in the wild. It is found in moist, well-drained areas including forest edges, shelterbelts, highway embankments, woodlands and old fields.

GROWTH: A multi-branched shrub up to 20 feet in height; it spreads by suckering and is sometimes seen in wide, tangled masses that can be 50 feet or more in width. Young twigs are green, turning gray and bumpy; as the branches mature, they develop two to four flat, wing-like bark extensions along the branches.

LEAVES: Oval leaves, 1 to 3 inches in length with a tapered base and a pointed tip grow oppositely on very short petioles (stemlets). Leaf edges are finely toothed; summer leaves are dull green on top, paler underneath. In fall, leaves gradually turn a vivid magenta-pink; it's common to see a leaf that is part green and part pink.

FRUIT: Egg-shaped, dull pink capsules, about ½ inch in length, grow on long stemlets from the leaf axils. Mature capsules split open to reveal seeds with a shiny, bright red coating. The fruits are inedible.

SEASON: Inconspicuous greenish flowers first appear in spring, and may be present through late summer. The pink capsules develop in late summer, splitting open in early fall.

COMPARE: Wahoo or burning bush (*E. atropurpureus*) is a native plant with similar leaves, growth form and fall color; however, the fruits are four-sided capsules that somewhat resemble a pinwheel, and the stems lack the wing-like extensions. Wahoo grows throughout Missouri and Illinois, and is also found in much of Iowa.

NOTES: When winged euonymus is in its fall color, it is a stunning plant; it's easy to see why it is frequently used as a landscape specimen. Unfortunately, its aggressive growth habits crowd out native plants, and it is considered invasive. Birds eat the seeds, helping to propagate the plant.

green = key identification feature   * specific MO locations not available

Winged
bark

LARGE SHRUB
OR SMALL TREE

ALTERNATE
LEAVES (TYP.)

SUMMER

* see below

Glossy Buckthorn (red stage)

Frangula alnus

HABITAT: Open woods, wetlands, abandoned fields. Also found along roads, on the edges of power line cuts, next to ponds and streams, and along paths. Tends to form thickets. Also called *Rhamnus frangula*.

GROWTH: A large shrub up to 20 feet in height; sometimes appears to be a small tree. Branches often droop down over paths, making the colorful fruits very obvious. The bark is smooth and grayish-brown, with noticeable lenticels (breathing pores) that are slightly raised.

LEAVES: Typically alternate, but may be opposite; smooth edges. Deep green above, lighter and slightly hairy below, with deep veins that form a V at the midrib, then curve near the edges to follow the contour of the leaf. Leaves are oval with a pointed tip, 2 to 4 inches long and one-half as wide, widest at the midpoint or slightly toward the tip.

FRUIT: The ¼-inch berries grow in the leaf axils; often seen as a pair, but may also be single or in small groups. They start out light green with a small dot at the base, developing a red blush before turning completely red. Glossy buckthorn are black at maturity (pg. 290), but are also included here, in the red section of this book, because they are so frequently seen in the red stage. The berries are mildly toxic.

SEASON: Fruits are on the plant from early through late summer. Green, red and black fruits may all be present on the plant at the same time.

COMPARE: Several other shrubs in our area have quantities of red fruit along the branches; the following pages help distinguish the species. Bush honeysuckle (pg. 150) have opposite leaves; fruits are translucent. Possumhaw and winterberry (pg. 158) have toothy leaves. Leaves of Carolina buckthorn (pg. 170) are glossy, up to 6 inches long and one-third as wide; edges are finely toothed. Fruits of autumn olive (pg. 160) are dotted with fine silver scales; the leaves are also silvery.

NOTES: This species was imported into the United States as an ornamental in the 1800s; it's quite attractive when the fruits first appear. It is considered invasive in many areas.

green = key identification feature

* specific IA locations not available

Green with red blush

LARGE SHRUB
OR SMALL TREE

ALTERNATE
LEAVES

MID SUMMER
TO FALL

Carolina Buckthorn

Frangula caroliniana

HABITAT: Moist, rocky areas, including bottomlands, ravines, dappled woodlands, streambanks, glades and thickets. It prefers partial shade, and is often found in the forest understory.

GROWTH: This native plant grows as a large shrub or small tree, up to 20 feet in height but typically shorter. It usually has multiple stems at its base and tends to be fairly open, but in areas of full sun, its growth becomes more dense. Twigs are greenish to reddish, turning gray with age; new growth is downy. The trunk is grayish-brown, often mottled with light patches; bark of old trunks often has vertical fissures.

LEAVES: The long oval leaves are almost lance-like; the bases are slightly rounded and the tip is pointed. Leaves grow alternately on pale ½-inch petioles (stemlets); the edges have very fine teeth. Leaves are 2 to 6 inches in length and one-third as wide. The top side is bright green, smooth and glossy, with distinct curving veins; undersides are paler and sometimes slightly hairy.

FRUIT: Round, opaque drupes, ¼ inch in diameter, grow on short stemlets from the leaf axils. Fruits are red most of the summer; most turn black in fall, but red fruits may be present even in fall. The fruit causes digestive upset; most sources consider it inedible.

SEASON: Small, yellowish-white flowers appear in spring. Fruits follow, and are red starting in midsummer; many turn black in fall.

COMPARE: Several other shrubs in our area have quantities of red fruit along the branches; the following pages help distinguish the species. Glossy buckthorn (pg. 168) has wide oval leaves that are 2 to 4 inches in length. Bush honeysuckle (pg. 150) have opposite leaves; fruits are translucent. Possumhaw and winterberry (pg. 158) have shorter leaves with a fine network of veins; possumhaw leaves are often wavy-edged. Fruits of autumn olive (pg. 160) are dotted with fine silver scales; the leaves are also silvery.

NOTES: Songbirds eat the fruits; deer browse on the twigs in winter.

green = key identification feature

Bark

TREE

ALTERNATE
LEAVES

EARLY TO MID
SUMMER

* see below

Mulberry

Morus alba, M. rubra

HABITAT: Two mulberries inhabit our area: the introduced white mulberry (*Morus alba*), and the less-common native red mulberry (*M. rubra*). Both are found in woodlands, fields, urban areas, and along fencelines and road ditches. White mulberry prefers sun, while red mulberry prefers shade and is found in deeper forests.

GROWTH: Medium to large trees; white mulberry is generally 25 to 40 feet high, while red mulberry can grow to 60 feet. Bark of older trees is brown and ridged; white mulberry bark has orange-colored areas between the ridges, while red mulberry bark is uniform in color. White mulberry stems are pinkish-brown; red mulberry's are light tan.

LEAVES: Alternate, with highly variable shape; some have irregular lobes, appearing mitten-like. White mulberry leaves are smooth, glossy, bright green and 3 to 4 inches long; edges have rounded teeth. Red mulberry leaves are rough-textured with hairy undersides, dark green and up to 10 inches long; edges have fine, pointed teeth.

FRUIT: A multiple fruit up to 1 inch long, composed of numerous drupes originating from a cluster of flowers. A short, soft stemlet remains attached to the picked fruit. Ripe white mulberry fruit may be white, but is more often pink, red or deep purple; red mulberries are blackish. Mulberries are sweet, and can be eaten raw or cooked. There are no toxic look-alikes; however, the fruit must be fully ripe and soft before eating, as unripe fruit and all other parts of the plant are mildly toxic.

SEASON: Fruits ripen in early to mid summer.

COMPARE: No tree resembles mulberries that are bearing fruit.

NOTES: Much confusing information exists about the differences between white and red mulberries. The information presented here relies on an excellent paper, *Red and White Mulberry in Indiana* (Sally S. Weeks; Purdue University). It's easy to identify a mulberry, but hard to determine exact species; however, the differences between them are less important to the forager than to the botanist.

green = key identification feature

* combined range

White mulberry tree and fruit

White mulberry bark

TREE | ALTERNATE LEAVES | SUMMER THROUGH FALL

* see below

Crabapple

Malus spp.

HABITAT: Numerous crabapple varieties are found in the wild throughout our region; they tend to hybridize, and exact identification is a matter for botanists. All produce edible fruits. Crabapples are found in a variety of habitats, including rich, moist woods, thickets, shelterbelts, abandoned ground, streambanks, urban parkland and grasslands.

GROWTH: A small to medium tree, with a rounded crown; may be as short as 5 feet, or as tall as 30 feet, generally with equal or greater spread. Stems and new growth are dark reddish-brown and shiny; older stems are gray and coarsely textured. All native crabapples have thorns, which may be blunt and rounded, or long and sharp; some domestic varieties have been bred to be thornless, and it is possible to encounter one of these escapees in the wild.

LEAVES: Oval leaves, tapered at both ends, grow alternately on long petioles (stemlets); they often grow in small clusters that alternate along the branch. Leaves are 1 to 5 inches in length, and generally one-third as wide; margins are toothy, but the teeth may be rounded or sharp depending on the species. Leaf surfaces may be smooth or hairy.

FRUIT: Rounded or slightly oval pomes, with a crown on the bottom, grow on a long stemlet. Depending on species, fruits may be yellow, orange, pink, red, or purple; size ranges from ½ to 1½ inches across. All crabapples are edible; some are bitter. There are no toxic look-alikes.

SEASON: Crabapples ripen from summer through fall.

COMPARE: Hawthorns (pg. 186) have fruit that appears similar, but leaves are more coarsely toothed and trees are thornier; fruits are generally oval, and tender when ripe. Cultivated apples (pg. 190) may escape into the wild, or may be found in an abandoned orchard; the leaves and growth habits are similar to crabapples, but fruit is larger.

NOTES: Eating quality varies from tree to tree, and also between species. Some crabapples have little flesh in proportion to the seeds; others are fleshy, sweet and juicy. Sample a few before harvesting.

green = key identification feature   * specific locations not available

TREE

ALTERNATE
LEAVES

SUMMER

Mahaleb -or- St. Lucie Cherry   *Prunus mahaleb*

HABITAT: Open woods, scrubby areas and thickets. It does well in low-quality soil; it prefers full sun, but tolerates some shade.

GROWTH: This non-native tree grows to 30 feet in height; it has an uneven, spreading, unkempt-looking crown and often appears weedy. Young stems are reddish-brown and smooth; older branches are gray, and the bark is rough in texture. All stems and branches are thornless, and are speckled with numerous lenticels (breathing pores).

LEAVES: Oval to heart-shaped leaves, with broad bases and pointed tips, 1½ to 2¾ inches in length; typically two-thirds as wide but sometimes almost round. The leaves grow alternately or in small clusters on pale green, half-inch petioles (stemlets). Edges are toothy; the top is dark green and moderately glossy, while the undersides are paler.

FRUIT: Smooth-skinned, rounded drupes, ¼ to ⅓ inch in diameter, containing rounded pits, grow on long stemlets originating in the leaf axils. The fruit is red in summer, eventually turning black if not consumed by birds. The flesh is bitter, and very thin in proportion to the pit; although edible, Mahaleb cherries are usually not collected for cooking. However, the fruits are used in Italy to prepare a traditional liqueur, and the dried pits are ground and used as a seasoning in the Mideast.

SEASON: Fruits are red in summer, turning black in late summer if still present on the tree.

COMPARE: Sour cherry (*P. cerasus*) rarely grows in the wild in our area; its leaves are longer and narrower. Fruits of this commercial species are larger, with much more flesh; they have an agreeably tart flavor, and are the traditional cherry used to make pie.

NOTES: Mahaleb cherry is frequently used as a rootstock for grafting commercial cherry cultivars. Cherry leaves, stems and pits contain hydrocyanic acid, a cyanide-producing compound. Leaves and pits should never be eaten, and care should be taken to avoid crushing pits when juicing the fruits. Cooking, drying or freezing eliminates the acid.

green = key identification feature

TREE

ALTERNATE LEAVES

MID TO LATE SUMMER

Pin Cherry –OR– Fire Cherry

Prunus pensylvanica

HABITAT: Clearings and edges in mixed-wood forests; hillsides; well-drained riverbanks; rock outcroppings. Prefers sunny sites. Pin cherry is one of the first plants to grow after a forest fire, giving rise to one of its common names, fire cherry.

GROWTH: A small native tree, sometimes appearing like a tall shrub; 3 to 25 feet in height, with an open form and a straight trunk. Bark is reddish-brown and smooth, with prominent raised lenticels (breathing pores); bark on older branches often peels off in horizontal strips.

LEAVES: Narrow, sharp-tipped leaves grow alternately from the stems on reddish petioles (stemlets); leaf edges have fine, rounded teeth. Leaves are 3 to 5 inches long, and roughly one-third as wide.

FRUIT: Round, shiny, bright red drupes, about ¼ inch across, grow from reddish stemlets in bunches along the stem. Fruits are translucent when ripe; the large pit can be seen as a shadow in the center of the fruit when the cherries are sunlit. Pin cherries are edible; they're sour when raw but make delicious jelly. There are no toxic look-alikes.

SEASON: Fruits ripen in mid to late summer; the foraging season is usually short because birds relish the cherries and can pick a tree clean of ripe fruit in a short time.

COMPARE: Black cherry (pg. 296) has similar narrow, toothy leaves, but fruits are blackish when ripe. The midrib of a black cherry leaf has reddish hairs near the base on the lower side; pin cherry leaves are hairless. Common chokecherries (pg. 154) have red fruits, but leaves are much wider; the fruits grow in racemes (long clusters).

NOTES: Pin cherry leaves and pits contain hydrocyanic acid, a cyanide-producing compound. The leaves and pits should never be eaten, and care should be taken to avoid crushing cherry pits when juicing the fruits. Cooking, drying or freezing eliminates the acid. Pin cherries have a pit that is large in proportion to the flesh, so pitting them for a pie would be a thankless task; they are usually juiced to prepare jelly.

green = key identification feature

TREE

ALTERNATE
LEAVES

MID TO LATE
SUMMER

American Wild Plum
Prunus americana

HABITAT: Mixed-wood and hardwood forests, particularly along the edges; pastures, thickets on the edges of cultivated areas, streamsides and hedgerows. Does best in full sun; will tolerate some shade.

GROWTH: A densely branching native tree with a broad crown, up 25 feet in height with equal spread but often much shorter. Main branches are stiff and dark reddish-brown, with numerous lenticels (breathing pores); many branches are armed with thorns. Older bark is reddish-gray, with a rough texture; it often comes off the tree in large plates.

LEAVES: Oval leaves that taper at both ends are 3 to 4 inches long and roughly one-third as wide; they grow alternately on fairly long petioles (stemlets). Edges are finely toothed; the tip is sharply pointed. Leaves are smooth and deep green above, paler below.

FRUIT: A fleshy, egg-shaped to round drupe with an oval pit, usually about 1 inch across. Fruits have a dusty bloom on the surface, and many have a slight vertical cleft. Ripe fruits are bright reddish-orange, with juicy, sweet, yellowish flesh. Fruits are edible raw or cooked; tastiness varies from plant to plant. There are no toxic look-alikes.

SEASON: White flowers appear in spring, before the leaves. Fruits ripen from mid through late summer.

COMPARE: Two other thorny native plum trees with red fruits inhabit our area. Chickasaw plum (*P. angustifolia*) is a smaller tree, often appearing shrub-like and forming dense thickets; its twigs are reddish and its leaves are folded along the midline. Canadian plum (*P. nigra*), a more northern species, has broader leaves; leaf teeth are blunt with small glands (visible with a lens). Mexican plum (pg. 212) is thorny, but ripe fruits are purplish-red. For information on thornless plums, see pg. 182.

NOTES: Plum leaves, stems and pits contain hydrocyanic acid, a cyanide-producing compound. The leaves and pits should never be eaten, and care should be taken to avoid crushing plum pits when juicing the fruits. Cooking, drying or freezing eliminates the acid.

green = key identification feature

DELICIOUS

Thorns on trunk

DELICIOUS

TREE

ALTERNATE
LEAVES

MID TO LATE
SUMMER

* see below

Goose Plum

Prunus hortulana, P. munsoniana

HABITAT: Two native plums in our area are called goose plum; to distinguish them, they are also called Hortulan plum (*Prunus hortulana*) and Munson's plum (*P. munsoniana*). Both grow in sunny areas with moist, well-drained soil; they are often seen along highways, fencerows and forest edges. In our area, Hortulan plum is more common; Munson's plum is found mostly in southern Missouri and Illinois.

GROWTH: Both grow to 20 feet in height, but are often shorter, shrubby-looking plants growing in dense thickets. Branches are dark brown, with numerous lenticels (breathing pores); older bark is reddish-gray, with a rough texture. Unlike many other wild plums, goose plums are thornless, although Hortulan plum twigs may have a spine on the end.

LEAVES: Elliptical, broadest towards the base, up to 5 inches in length. Leaves of Munson's plum are narrow, about one-quarter as wide as they are long, and many have visible reddish glands on the underside along the teeth; leaves of Hortulan plum are shorter and broader, and tend to fold sharply along the midline. Both grow alternately on fairly long petioles (stemlets). Edges are finely toothed; the tip is sharply pointed. Leaves are smooth and deep green above, paler below.

FRUIT: A fleshy, egg-shaped to round drupe, ¾ to 1 inch across with a slight vertical cleft and an oval pit. Ripe Munson's plums are bright red; Hortulan may be red or yellow. Both are edible raw or cooked; tastiness varies from plant to plant. There are no toxic look-alikes.

SEASON: Munson's plum produces masses of white flowers in early spring, before leaves appear. Hortulan plum flowers a bit later, after the leaves have formed. Fruits of both are ripe in mid to late summer.

COMPARE: Some wild plums have thorns; see pgs. 180 and 212.

NOTES: Plum leaves, stems and pits contain hydrocyanic acid, a cyanide-producing compound. The leaves and pits should never be eaten, and care should be taken to avoid crushing plum pits when juicing the fruits. Cooking, drying or freezing eliminates the acid.

green = key identification feature   * combined range

Munson's plum

TREE

OPPOSITE
LEAVES

LATE
SUMMER

Flowering Dogwood

Cornus florida

HABITAT: This native tree is found in areas with cool, moist, well-drained soil; it is common in the understory of hardwood and mixed-wood forests. It prefers ample sunlight, although it will grow in partial shade.

GROWTH: A small tree, typically 25 feet in height or less, with equal or greater width. The tree produces branches fairly close to the ground; they continue up the trunk in a layered fashion. Twigs are green to purplish, and finely hairy; the trunk has dark brownish-gray bark that is broken into square patches, somewhat similar to the persimmon tree (pg. 88). Masses of flowers with four large, white, petal-like bracts appear in spring, before the tree has leafed out.

LEAVES: Oval leaves, 3 to 5 inches in length and half as wide, grow oppositely on short, grooved petioles (stemlets); the base is tapered and the tip is sharply pointed. Leaves are smooth-edged, or may have very fine teeth (visible with a lens); edges are often slightly wavy. The veins are prominent, curving to follow the leaf edge. Leaves are dark green most of the summer, developing maroon blotches in late summer and turning mottled red in early fall. When a leaf is pulled apart, fine white threads remain between the leaf pieces.

FRUIT: Tight clusters of shiny, bright red, football-shaped drupes grow at the branch tips; each is ⅓ to ½ inch in length and one-third as wide. A black floral remnant is present at the tip. The fruit is very bitter when raw; although it is not toxic, most references consider it inedible.

SEASON: Fruits are green in early summer, ripening to red in late summer; they may persist through winter if not eaten by birds.

COMPARE: Leaves of flowering dogwood resemble other members of the *Cornus* family, but with its distinctive flowers, bright red fruits and lovely fall color, flowering dogwood is easy to recognize.

NOTES: Flowering dogwood is Missouri's state tree. The fruits are an important winter food source for birds including quail, waxwings, wild turkeys, robins and cardinals; deer browse on the leaves and twigs.

green = key identification feature

TREE

ALTERNATE
LEAVES

MIDSUMMER
THROUGH FALL

Hawthorn

Crataegus spp.

HABITAT: Over three dozen species of hawthorn are found in the wild in our area; they hybridize frequently, and identification of exact species in the wild is a matter for specialists. Hawthorns inhabit rocky areas, pastures, old fields and woodlots, sun-dappled mixed-wood forests, and shelterbelts. Trees in sunny areas produce the most fruit.

GROWTH: Small to medium trees, occasionally appearing as large shrubs; height varies wildly, from 6 feet to over 40 feet. Hawthorns often have a rounded crown and widely spreading branches. Thorns—often long and sharp, as in the photo at right—are always present on native wild hawthorns, but may be negligible or absent on cultivated varieties which have escaped into the wild. Bark on the main trunk is usually dark gray and roughly textured, with vertical fissures; young stems are smooth and gray-brown.

LEAVES: Hawthorn leaves are sharply toothed, although specific shape is variable. The most easily identifiable hawthorns have leaves that are broadly tapered and smooth-edged at the base, with coarse, sharp teeth from the end of the base to the tip. Some species have toothy lobes; others are oval, like crabapple leaves but with larger, sharper teeth. Leaves are typically 2 to 4 inches long, and grow alternately.

FRUIT: Pomes, generally oval with slightly flattened sides; they have a crown on the bottom and grow on a long stemlet. Fruits are generally reddish when ripe, but may be yellowish; size ranges from ¼ to 1 inch across. All hawthorns are edible; there are no toxic look-alikes.

SEASON: Hawthorns ripen from midsummer through early fall.

COMPARE: Crabapples (pg. 174) are similar, but leaves are more reliably oval-shaped, with finer, rounded teeth; their fruit is generally rounder.

NOTES: Before harvesting hawthorns, taste a few from the tree you're considering. The best hawthorns have a fair amount of juicy flesh in proportion to the seeds; flesh may be soft and tender, or crunchy like an apple, and the flavor is often reminiscent of pears.

green = key identification feature

TREE

ALTERNATE
COMPOUND
LEAVES

LATE SUMMER
THROUGH FALL

Smooth

Staghorn

Smooth Sumac
–AND– Staghorn Sumac

Rhus glabra, R. typhina

HABITAT: Sunny fields and fence rows, disturbed areas, road ditches and embankments, waste ground.

GROWTH: A small native tree, sometimes appearing as a large shrub, generally 10 to 15 feet in height. Sumac spreads readily via underground rhizomes (root-bearing stems), and is usually seen in dense colonies. Smooth sumac (*Rhus glabra*) has smooth twigs and leafstalks; those of staghorn sumac (*R. typhina*) are covered with fine, dense hairs. Bark is dark and smooth on both species.

LEAVES: Pinnately (feather-like) compound leaves, each with 11 to 31 leaflets, grow alternately. Leaves are 12 to 24 inches long. Leaflets are 2 to 5 inches long, lance-shaped with toothy edges; deep green on top, paler underneath. Leafstalks of smooth sumac are reddish; those of staghorn sumac are greenish to tan. Leaves turn red in fall.

FRUIT: Large, cone-shaped clusters of fuzzy, reddish-orange drupes grow upright at the end of the branches, rising above the leaves. Smooth sumac has clusters that are irregular; often, two or three clusters of various sizes grow side-by-side at the end of the branch. Staghorn sumac has a single, fairly symmetrical cluster at the end of the branch. Clusters are typically 3 to 6 inches long. The drupes are lemony-sour, and can be used to make a lemonade-type beverage. There are no toxic look-alikes that have reddish-orange fruits.

SEASON: Sumac clusters ripen in late summer, and persist on the plant through winter, although their flavor is washed away by fall rains.

COMPARE: Winged sumac (pg. 210) is similar in overall appearance, but the leafstalk has green wing-like extensions between the leaflets; its fruit clusters are purplish in the summer, ripening to red in fall.

NOTES: The fruits have tiny hairs that are somewhat irritating to the throat; strain your sumac lemonade through a coffee filter to remove them.

green = key identification feature

Smooth sumac

Staghorn sumac

TREE

ALTERNATE
LEAVES

LATE SUMMER
TO FALL

* see below

Apple

Malus pumila

HABITAT: This Asian import is sometimes found in the wild in our area in abandoned orchards and on old homestead sites; they are also found occasionally in areas where apple cores have been discarded by hikers, picnickers, anglers and the like. Apples may also grow in the wild near areas where people feed apples to wildlife, or where hunters use apples to attract deer or bears. Apple trees produce more fruit in moderate to full sun, and require adequate moisture.

GROWTH: A sturdy, multi-branched tree, usually with a full, rounded crown. Young branches are downy but smooth and reddish-brown, with numerous lenticels (breathing pores); older bark is rough and gray, often peeling off in scaly patches.

LEAVES: Oval leaves that are coarsely textured grow alternately on long, downy petioles (stemlets); leaves are typically 2 to 3 inches in length and half as wide, with a rounded or tapering base and a pointed tip. Edges have small, sharp teeth. Top sides are dark green; undersides are paler and densely hairy.

FRUIT: The familiar apple is often misshapen and scarred when found in the wild. Ripe fruits are red, or yellowish with an overall red blush. The skin is smooth and usually dotted with pale speckles; feral apples often have coarse brown or yellowish blotches on the skin. They are edible, with no toxic look-alikes; eating quality varies from tree to tree.

SEASON: Apple trees produce fragrant white flowers in spring. Like their domestic forbears, feral apples ripen in late summer to fall.

COMPARE: Crabapples (pg. 174) are much more common in the wild; they vary dramatically in color and size, but basically look like small apples.

NOTES: Feral apples can be delicious, or tart and astringent. It's possible to discover the remnants of a cultivar that has faded from commercial use; some of these old varieties were used to make cider, or had other specific uses. If the apple has minor insect damage, simply cut away the affected portion, and enjoy the rest of the apple raw or cooked.

green = key identification feature

* specific locations not available

TREE

ALTERNATE
LEAVES

LATE SUMMER
TO FALL

Cucumber-tree

Umbrella-tree

* see below

Cucumber-tree
–AND– Umbrella-tree

Magnolia acuminata, M. tripetala

HABITAT: These native trees prefer mountainous or hilly areas with rich, moist, well-drained soil. They are found scattered in well-drained bottomlands, along streambanks and on cool hillsides. They prefer light shade. Umbrella-tree is not found in the wild in Illinois or Iowa.

GROWTH: Cucumber-tree is the larger of the two species, attaining heights up to 80 feet; umbrella-tree grows to 40 feet in height, and tends to have a more spreading crown. The bark of the cucumber-tree is rough and flaky; bark of the umbrella-tree is smooth, with scattered warty lenticels (breathing pores), similar to other magnolias.

LEAVES: Large, smooth, bright green leaves which are broadly oval, with pointed tips; leaf edges are smooth, and may appear slightly wavy. Cucumber-tree leaves are up to 10 inches in length and one-half as wide, growing alternately along the branches on long, fleshy petioles (stemlets); leaf bases are broad. Umbrella-tree leaves are up to 20 inches in length and about one-third as wide, growing on petioles in clusters at the ends of the branches; leaf bases are tapered.

FRUIT: Both trees produce a fleshy, inedible fruit that resembles a narrow green pineapple when young. Umbrella-tree fruit is 4 to 6 inches in length and stays fairly symmetrical, ripening to pink. Cucumber-tree fruit starts out symmetrical, but quickly becomes misshapen while still green; the ripe, reddish fruit appears swollen and knobby. In fall, both fruits split open to release red seeds; cucumber-tree sometimes does not split to release its seeds, eventually falling to the ground whole.

SEASON: Green fruits are present most of the summer, ripening in late summer to early fall; the fruits split and release seeds in fall.

COMPARE: Other magnolia trees have similar leaves, fruits and growth habits, but are not found in the wild in our area.

NOTES: Birds and other wildlife eat the seeds that develop in the ripe fruit.

green = key identification feature   * specific MO locations not available

Cucumber-tree (ripe)

Cucumber-tree (green)

Umbrella-tree (ripe)

Umbrella-tree (seeds)

TENDER
LEAFY PLANT

ALTERNATE
COMPOUND
LEAVES

LATE SUMMER
TO FALL

American Spikenard

Aralia racemosa

HABITAT: This native plant is found in rich, open deciduous and mixed-wood forests, thickets, wooded slopes and ravines. It prefers moist, well-drained soil, and grows in full sun to part shade.

GROWTH: A very large, bushy, somewhat top-heavy plant that is almost shrublike and grows from an underground rhizome (root-bearing stem). Typically 3 to 5 feet in height, with equal width near the top; white flowers grow in numerous long, loose, upright clusters that have an overall conical shape. Stems are soft and greenish-purple, with fine hairs.

LEAVES: Large doubly compound leaves, each with three divisions, grow alternately on the stems; overall leaf length is up to 3 feet. Each of the three divisions has three to five heart-shaped leaflets that are 3 to 6 inches in length and two-thirds as wide, with doubly toothed edges and a pointed tip. Leaflets are green and slightly hairy on both surfaces; leaflet nodes are often purplish.

FRUIT: Round drupes, each up to ¼ inch across, replace the flowers in the long, loose clusters (racemes); drupes are greenish when young, ripening to reddish-purple. The effect is that of a long column of tiny grapes. The fruits have a sharp, unpleasant aftertaste; although a few sources list them as edible, most say they should not be eaten.

SEASON: Spikenard flowers in mid to late summer; fruits ripen from late summer to fall.

COMPARE: Bristly sarsaparilla (*A. hispida*) is similar in appearance, but smaller overall, with much smaller leaves; its stems are covered with bristly hairs, and its fruits grow in rounded clusters rather than long racemes. All parts of the plant have an unpleasant odor. Fruits of bristly sarsaparilla are not edible.

NOTES: Like its much smaller relative sarsaparilla (pg. 244), spikenard has aromatic, spicy-flavored rhizomes that are often used as a flavoring agent. The young shoot tips can also be cooked as a vegetable.

green = key identification feature

WOODY
VINE

ALTERNATE
LEAVES

LATE SUMMER
TO EARLY FALL

• see below

Wild Grape (several)

Vitis spp.

HABITAT: Six native wild grape species grow in our area. Riverbank grapes (*Vitis riparia*) grow everywhere in our region except south-central Missouri. Frost grapes *(V. vulpina)* are found throughout Missouri and Illinois, as well as in eastern Iowa. Summer (*V. aestivalis*) and winter (*V. cinerea*) grapes are common in southern Illinois and most of Missouri. Catbird or red grapes (*V. palmata*) are found in Missouri and Illinois, primarily in counties bordering the Mississippi River. Sand grapes *(V. rupestris)* grow in southern Missouri. All inhabit moist, rich areas including tangles, thickets, river and stream banks and woodland margins; they do best in full sun.

GROWTH: Grapes are woody vines, with flexible stems and rough bark on the trunks; all listed here except sand grape are 30 feet or longer and use tendrils to climb. Sand grape is a sprawling, shrub-like vine that is usually shorter than 8 feet; it has tendrils only at the stem ends.

LEAVES: Toothy leaves grow alternately on long petioles (stemlets). Red grape leaves are deeply lobed with five fingers; the others are generally heart-shaped with shallow lobes or no lobes, although summer grape may have a few deeply lobed leaves. Undersides of summer and winter grape leaves are white and downy; frost, red and riverbank have hairs underneath only on the veins, while sand grape is hairless.

FRUIT: Clusters of edible round, juicy berries hang from the vine on separate stalks, opposite a leaf. Frost, winter and red grapes are about ¼ inch across; summer and sand grapes, up to ½ inch. Riverbank grapes are about ⅜ inch across and bluish-purple; the others are dark purple to blackish. All have a dusty whitish bloom, and one to six seeds.

SEASON: Grapes ripen in late summer to early fall.

COMPARE: Grapes may be confused with several inedible or toxic fruits; please see "Be certain, be safe: Wild grapes" on pg. 22.

NOTES: All true wild grapes are edible; fruits from individual plants may be sour or sweet, regardless of variety.

green = key identification feature   * combined range

Riverbank grapes

WOODY
VINE

ALTERNATE
LEAVES

LATE SUMMER
TO EARLY FALL

Canada Moonseed

Menispermum canadense

HABITAT: Stream banks, thickets, moist woody areas. Prefers full sun.

GROWTH: This native woody vine reaches up to 20 feet in length. Unlike wild grapes (pg. 196), moonseed has no tendrils, and climbs by coiling its central stem around the host. Younger stems are hairy, greenish or reddish and flexible; older stems are smooth, bronze to dark reddish-brown and woody.

LEAVES: Alternate, with three to seven shallow lobes; edges are smooth and untoothed. The long petiole (stemlet) is attached to the underside of the leaf, slightly away from the base (peltate). The upper surface is smooth and light green; the underside is silvery-green with fine hairs. Leaves are 4 to 7 inches long, and equally wide.

FRUIT: Purplish-blue to purplish-black drupes with a whitish bloom, each containing a single flat seed shaped like a broad crescent (a circle with a bite taken away). Drupes are round and ¼ to ⅓ inch across; they grow in loose clusters that hang from the vine on a long, spindly fruit stalk, opposite a leaf. They are highly toxic.

SEASON: Moonseed fruits are ripe in late summer to early fall, at about the same time as wild grapes.

COMPARE: Moonseed bears an unfortunate resemblance to wild grapes (pg. 196). However, the leaves of wild grapes have toothy edges, and are attached directly to the petiole; those of moonseed have smooth edges and peltate attachment. Grapes have one to six small, oval or pear-shaped seeds, rather than the single crescent-shaped seed that gives moonseed its common name. Finally, grapes attach themselves to hosts by using tendrils, which are absent on moonseed. It is very important to pay strict attention when harvesting wild grapes, to avoid gathering any moonseed fruits, which are toxic.

NOTES: Moonseed fruits contain the alkaloid dauricine, a compound that affects the heart. Its use in medicine is being studied, but it is toxic in its natural form as found in moonseed.

green = key identification feature

Fruits and seed

WOODY
VINE

ALTERNATE
LEAVES

LATE SUMMER
THROUGH FALL

Heartleaf Peppervine
–OR– Raccoon Grape

Ampelopsis cordata

HABITAT: This native woody vine is common in the southern half of our region; it is found in rich, moist, well-drained areas including river and stream banks, alongside highways and rural roads, woodland margins, pond edges and waste ground. It grows in sun or partial shade.

GROWTH: A vining plant that can grow to 60 feet in length; it uses its occasional branched tendrils and a twining habit to climb other plants, fences, poles or buildings. Young stems are green and flexible, with slightly angled edges; older stems are brown and woody, with raised, bumpy lenticels (breathing pores). The trunk is often several inches in diameter; it has non-shredding brown bark with long ridges.

LEAVES: Heart-shaped leaves with a broad, flat base grow alternately from the vine on a petiole (stemlet) that is almost as long as the leaf. Edges have coarse, sharp teeth. Leaves are up to 5 inches in length, and nearly as wide at the base; the tip is sharply pointed.

FRUIT: Loose, wide clusters of speckled berries hang from the vine on a thin fruit stalk, opposite a leaf. Berries are about ¼ inch across and are round or slightly flattened; they may be maroon, purple, blue, orangish or pink—all on the same plant, at the same time. The fruits are inedible.

SEASON: Berries mature from late summer through fall.

COMPARE: Porcelainberry (*A. brevipedunculata*), an introduced plant that is related to heartleaf peppervine, is found in our area only occasionally in Illinois; its leaves have noticeable lobes. Porcelainberry and heartleaf peppervine both have some similarities to wild grapes (pg. 196), but grapes grow in tighter, longer clusters; grapes are unspeckled, with a dusty bloom, and the stems have no lenticels.

NOTES: Heartleaf peppervine is often seen in masses along freeway fences and climbing over other plants. Birds eat the berries, helping to spread the plant.

green = key identification feature

SMALL
WOODY SHRUB

 ALTERNATE
LEAVES

 MID TO LATE
SUMMER

• see below

Smooth –or– Swamp Gooseberry *Ribes hirtellum*

HABITAT: Rocky shorelines, clearings, boggy areas, and moist woods, especially those along rivers or ponds.

GROWTH: An arching native shrub about 3 feet high. Mature stems are finely hairy but not bristly; young stems have scattered bristles. Leaf nodes have one to three thorns that are ⅓ inch or less in length.

LEAVES: Attached alternately to the stem by a petiole (stemlet); each leaf node has one to three leaves. Each leaf has three to five distinct lobes, resembling a maple leaf with rounded teeth. The leaves are slightly hairy on both surfaces.

FRUIT: The smooth, ¼- to ½-inch round berry grows on a thin stemlet from leaf nodes, singly or in clusters of two or three. Distinct stripes run longitudinally on the berry; a prominent flower remnant, often called a pigtail, is present at the end of the berry. Smooth gooseberries are green when young, maturing to purple or purplish-black when ripe. Gooseberries are edible in both the green and ripe stages.

SEASON: Ripe fruits are present from mid to late summer.

COMPARE: Two other native gooseberries inhabit our region, but they are easy to distinguish. Ripe fruits of prickly gooseberry (pg. 136) are reddish-purple and bear small, soft prickles, especially on the half closest to the stem; ripe fruits of Missouri gooseberry (pg. 264) are black, with smooth skins. Stems of Missouri gooseberry have scattered thin bristles, which are also often present on prickly gooseberry stems. Currant shrubs (pgs. 134, 266) resemble gooseberry shrubs, but berries are typically borne in racemes (long clusters of multiple fruits).

NOTES: Ripe gooseberries are excellent in baked desserts, sauces and other dishes. Green gooseberries (pg. 54) are rich in pectin, and are used primarily for jam and jelly. Smooth gooseberry is considered endangered in Illinois.

green = key identification feature

LARGE
WOODY SHRUB

OPPOSITE
COMPOUND
LEAVES

LATE
SUMMER

Common Elderberry

Sambucus canadensis

HABITAT: This native shrub grows in moist areas such as river and stream banks, woodland edges, shelterbelts, thickets, abandoned fields, roadsides, meadows, and ditch edges. It prefers full sun to part shade.

GROWTH: An open shrub, 5 to 12 feet in height, with a broad, rounded crown. Branches are yellowish-gray, with numerous warty lenticels (breathing pores); older bark is yellowish-brown or gray, streaked with white. White flowers grow in large, showy umbrella-like clusters; stemlets are reddish. When the flowers fall and berries are developing, the plant is easy to spot because of the groupings of rounded, purplish flower stemlets, which have a lacy appearance.

LEAVES: Compound leaves, each with five to 11 leaflets, grow oppositely on the stem; leaves are 6 to 10 inches long and nearly as wide. Leaflets are 2 to 4 inches long and one-half as wide, broadly oval and tapered on both ends; edges are sharply toothed. The top sides are dark green and smooth; the undersides are paler and may be downy.

FRUIT: Round berries, about 3/16 inch in diameter with three to five seeds, grow in drooping, flat-topped clusters (cymes). Berries are green when immature, ripening to deep purple or purplish-black; stemlets are reddish-purple. The berries are edible, and are juiced to make jelly, jam and wine. Leaves, stems, seeds and all other parts of all elderberry species are toxic. Common elderberry might be confused with red elderberry (pg. 148); which is rare in our area. See below for more information about this plant; its berries are inedible.

SEASON: Flowers appear in early summer; fruits ripen in late summer.

COMPARE: Red elderberry (pg. 148) has similar growth and leaves, but berries are bright red and grow in rounded clusters, rather than the flat-topped clusters of common elderberry. Red elderberry ripens a month or more before common elderberry.

NOTES: Some sources list this plant as *Sambucus nigra* var. *canadensis*. The flowers are used to make wine, and also a tea to treat headache.

green = key identification feature

LARGE SHRUB
OR SMALL TREE

OPPOSITE
LEAVES

EARLY
SUMMER

Eastern Swamp Privet

Forestiera acuminata

HABITAT: Low, wet areas such as swamps, sloughs, bottomland forests and bayous; also found along streams, lakes and ponds. It grows in areas with full sun to moderate shade, and can survive sustained flooding during the growing season.

GROWTH: This native plant is a large shrub or small tree, up to 30 feet in height but usually shorter. It has an unkempt, straggly appearance, with an open crown. Young branches are smooth and light brown, with numerous pale lenticels (breathing pores); twig tips sometimes have a spine at the end. Older branches are gray; the trunk has dark brown bark that is smooth or slightly ridged. Swamp privet is usually unisexual—a plant is either male or female, and each produces a different type of flower. Typically, only female plants bear fruit.

LEAVES: Glossy, smooth, yellowish-green leaves, 2 to 4 inches in length and one-half as wide, grow oppositely on ½-inch petioles (stemlets) that have flattened edges. The leaves are widest at the midpoint, with a sharply pointed tip and a base that tapers to a V; the overall impression is that of a round-sided diamond. Edges are slightly toothy above the midpoint. The undersides are pale and have scattered fine hairs on the veins.

FRUIT: An elongated, lightly textured oval drupe, up to ¾ inch in length, that is purple or purplish-black when ripe. A few sources consider the fruits edible; however, the drupes are very thin-fleshed and are generally regarded as inedible.

SEASON: Masses of yellow flowers appear in spring, before the plants have leafed out. Fruits develop in late spring; they ripen in early summer and often fall off the plant, or are eaten by birds, shortly after.

COMPARE: European and border privet (pg. 284) have opposite leaves and dark fruit, but the leaves are not diamond-shaped and lack the sharply pointed tip; fruits tend to cluster at the ends of the branches.

NOTES: The fruits are relished by waterfowl and other birds.

green = key identification feature

LARGE SHRUB OR SMALL TREE

ALTERNATE LEAVES

EARLY TO MID SUMMER

• see below

Serviceberry (several)

Amelanchier spp.

HABITAT: Six serviceberry varieties are native to our area; all produce edible fruits which look similar. Found in mixed-wood forests and thickets. They may grow as a single specimen, or in groups. Low serviceberry (*Amelanchier humilis*; also called shadbush) and running serviceberry (*A. stolonifera*) spread by runners (horizontal stems), and form colonies; running serviceberry is more likely to grow on **extremely rocky areas**.

GROWTH: An erect shrub or small tree, usually 3 to 15 feet tall; smooth serviceberry (*A. laevis*) may grow to **30 feet**. Bark is smooth, and usually gray or brownish; older bark may have vertical furrows. Roundleaf serviceberry (*A. sanguinea*) has **reddish twigs and branches**.

LEAVES: Alternate, 1 to 3 inches in length, with long petioles (stemlets). Leaf edges of running, smooth, downy (*A. arborea*) and inland (*A. interior*) are **finely toothed**; running has leaves that are nearly circular and lack teeth on the bottom half, while smooth, downy and inland leaves are **heart-shaped**. Inland has a very short pointed tip, while the pointed tips on smooth and downy are long. Downy is **densely hairy** underneath, particularly on young leaves. Low serviceberry leaves have coarse teeth on the upper half; roundleaf has coarse teeth around the entire leaf, which is nearly circular.

FRUIT: A ½-inch round pome with a **crown on the base**, resembling a blueberry or a tiny apple, on a long stemlet; fruits grow along a separate fruiting stalk and have a whitish bloom. Most are sweet and delicious; the tiny, soft seeds are unnoticeable. Ripe fruits range from reddish-purple, to bluish-purple, to black; judge ripeness by texture, and choose soft fruits to harvest. There are no toxic look-alikes.

SEASON: Fruits are ripe from early to mid summer, depending on species and location.

COMPARE: Chokecherries (pg. 154) have similar leaves, but the fruits grow in racemes (long clusters of multiple fruits).

NOTES: Also called Juneberry, a reference to its blooming time.

green = key identification feature   * combined range

LARGE SHRUB
OR SMALL TREE

ALTERNATE
COMPOUND
LEAVES

LATE SUMMER
THROUGH FALL

* see below

Winged –or- Shining Sumac
Rhus copallinum

HABITAT: This native plant is found in fields and disturbed areas, alongside roads, in open woods and sandy areas, and on rocky outcrops. It prefers sun, and can tolerate drought.

GROWTH: A large, open shrub or small tree, ranging from 3 to 20 feet in height. Sumac spreads readily via underground rhizomes (root-bearing stems), and is usually seen in dense colonies. Twigs are reddish-brown to gray, with numerous lenticels (breathing pores); young twigs are downy. Older bark is gray to brown, with a rough texture. Dense clusters of tiny yellowish flowers grow upright from the end of the branch; the flowers are present from late spring through late summer.

LEAVES: Pinnately (feather-like) compound leaves, each with seven to 15 leaflets (some accounts say up to 23), grow alternately. Leaves are up to 12 inches in length. Leaflets are 1 to 3 inches in length and lance-shaped; they are glossy and deep green on top, paler and downy underneath. Edges are typically smooth, although some fine teeth may be present. Leafstalks have flat, wing-like green extensions between the leaflets. Leaves turn brilliant red in fall.

FRUIT: Cone-shaped clusters of fuzzy, sticky purplish or pink drupes develop at the end of the branches starting in midsummer; the drupes turn red in late summer to fall. Clusters are 3 to 5 inches in length; the weight of the fruit typically causes the cluster to droop. The drupes are lemony-sour, and can be used to make a lemonade-type beverage. There are no toxic look-alikes that have purplish, pink or red fruits.

SEASON: Sumac clusters ripen in late summer through fall, and persist on the plant through winter; their flavor is washed away by fall rains.

COMPARE: Smooth and staghorn sumac (pg. 188) are similar in overall appearance, but their leafstalks lack the wings; underripe fruits are orange, not purple, and the fruit clusters stand upright.

NOTES: The fruits have tiny hairs that are somewhat irritating to the throat; strain your sumac lemonade through a coffee filter to remove them.

green = key identification feature   * specific IA locations not available

Pink cluster

TREE

ALTERNATE
LEAVES

MID TO LATE
SUMMER

• see below

Mexican Plum

Prunus mexicana

HABITAT: This native plum is found in areas with rich, moist soil, including roadsides, pastures, river bottoms, streamsides and hedgerows. It does best in full sun, but will tolerate some shade.

GROWTH: A medium-sized tree, up to 30 feet in height with equal spread; unlike many other wild plums, it does not form thickets. Branches are smooth and reddish-brown, with numerous lenticels (breathing pores); many branches become thorny as they mature. Older bark is gray, with a rough texture; it often comes off the tree in curled strips, revealing orangish wood underneath.

LEAVES: Oval, broadest around the midpoint, up to 5 inches in length and one-half as wide. Leaves grow alternately on fairly long petioles (stemlets), which are densely hairy on emerging leaves. Edges have moderately fine teeth; the tip is sharply pointed. Leaves are smooth and deep green above, paler below; veins on the underside are hairy.

FRUIT: A fleshy, round to egg-shaped drupe, typically 1 inch across but sometimes larger. Fruits have a dusty bloom on the surface, and many have a slight vertical cleft. Ripe fruits are purplish-red, with juicy, sweet, yellowish flesh. Fruits are edible raw or cooked; tastiness varies from plant to plant. There are no toxic look-alikes

SEASON: Fragrant white flowers bloom in profusion in early spring, before the leaves appear. Fruits are yellow when immature, turning mauve and finally ripening to purplish-red in mid to late summer.

COMPARE: Several other thorny plum trees, including the common American wild plum (*P. americana*), grow in our area, but their ripe fruits are red; please see pg. 180 for more information. Goose plums (pg. 182) are thornless; ripe fruits are red or yellow.

NOTES: Plum leaves, stems and pits contain hydrocyanic acid, a cyanide-producing compound. The leaves and pits should never be eaten, and care should be taken to avoid crushing plum pits when juicing the fruits. Cooking, drying or freezing eliminates the acid.

green = key identification feature   * specific IA locations not available

Ripening fruits

Ripe fruits

TREE

ALTERNATE
LEAVES

FALL

Water Tupelo

Nyssa aquatica

HABITAT: Swamps, sloughs and floodplains; it will grow in areas where its root system is flooded for much of the year, and does best in soil that is saturated most of the growing season. They require ample sun.

GROWTH: A large, native tree, up to 100 feet in height; the trunk can be several feet across at the base. Twigs are yellowish to reddish-brown; older branches are dark reddish-brown, and the trunk is gray, often with scaly ridges, warty patches or plates. Mature trees are typically wider at the base than the rest of the trunk, giving them a swollen appearance. When the ground is dry, roots may sometimes be seen growing up out of the soil.

LEAVES: Oblong leaves are 4 to 8 inches in length, and about one-half as wide; the bases are tapered, and the tip is pointed. The leaf edges are smooth, although leaves may have one or more large, pointed teeth. Leaves grow alternately on 1- to 3-inch petioles (stemlets) which are typically yellowish-green and tinged with red. The midrib is pale; veins are prominent on the underside.

FRUIT: Teardrop-shaped drupes grow on long stalks from leaf nodes. The drupes are 1 to 1½ inches in length and one-third as wide. They are dark green when immature, ripening to a dusky purple; they have light speckles, and a small nub at the bottom. The skin is thick and tough; the pit inside is heavily ribbed. The fruits are bitter but edible; they are sometimes called Ogeechee lime, a name that is more appropriate for the fruits of the related Ogeechee tupelo (*N. ogeche*), a smaller tree that grows in the extreme southeast.

SEASON: The fruits develop in early summer and are ripe in fall.

COMPARE: Blackgum (pg. 242) is a related tree, but its leaves are much smaller, and it grows in areas that are not flooded.

NOTES: The flowers are attractive to bees, and tupelo honey is a well-known epicurean delight. Ducks and other birds, as well as deer, squirrels and raccoons, eat the fruits.

green = key identification feature

TENDER
LEAFY PLANT

ALTERNATE
LEAVES

MID TO
LATE SUMMER

Smooth Solomon's Seal · *Polygonatum biflorum*

HABITAT: Rich, moist mixed-wood and deciduous forests, waste ground, urban areas, roadside ditches, thickets, edges of streams and ponds.

GROWTH: This native plant grows as a single stem in a long arch from the underground rhizome (root-bearing stem). Smooth Solomon's seal is the largest of the Solomon's seal family, and is often called great Solomon's seal because of its size. The stem can grow up to 5 feet in length, although it is usually much shorter; longer stems arch gracefully, making the plant appear shorter than it is.

LEAVES: Lance-shaped leaves with many parallel veins grow alternately, attached directly to the stem or slightly clasping; leaves are 2 to 7 inches in length and are typically narrow. Topsides are green and smooth; undersides are paler, with hairless veins. Leaves are broadest near the base, tapering to a point; edges are smooth and hairless.

FRUIT: Round, dark blue berries, about ⅓ inch across with a slight vertical cleft, grow in small groups or singly from the leaf axils. Berries have a slight bloom, and grow from thin stemlets. They are inedible.

SEASON: Berries mature in mid to late summer.

COMPARE: The only other "true" Solomon's seal that grows in our area is hairy Solomon's seal (*P. pubescens*). Like smooth Solomon's seal, berries of hairy Solomon's seal grow from the leaf axils; however, the plant is shorter, generally 3 feet or less in length, and leaves grow on short petioles (stemlets); edges of the leaf, and leaf veins on the undersides, have fine hairs, and there are only one to four berries at each leaf axil. All other Solomon's seals in our area are "false," having the berries growing from the tip of the stem. Please see the common false Solomon's seal text on pg. 36 for more information about plants with similar appearance.

NOTES: The rhizome of smooth Solomon's seal is edible when cooked; however, the plant is protected in much of its range and should be harvested only where abundant (and legal).

green = key identification feature

Overview of plant

TENDER
LEAFY PLANT

OPPOSITE
COMPOUND
LEAVES

MID TO
LATE SUMMER

Blue Cohosh
Caulophyllum thalictroides

HABITAT: Rich, moist mixed-wood and deciduous forests, valleys, river bottoms and floodplains. Grows best in shade or dappled sun.

GROWTH: A leafy, native plant that grows from an underground rhizome (root-bearing stem). The main stem divides into two stems, each with compound leaves that are sub-divided into three stalks. Stalks on the lower leaf each have three to nine leaflets. The upper leaf is smaller; each stalk typically has three leaflets. A separate, leafless flowering stalk rises above the leaves. Blue cohosh is typically 12 to 18 inches in height, but it can reach 3 feet. It often forms colonies.

LEAVES: Blue cohosh has many leaves, that grow in a complex pattern as described above. Individual leaflets are typically tulip-shaped and have rounded lobes ending in a shallow point, generally three lobes per leaflet but sometimes two. Leaves are up to 12 inches long; individual leaflets are 1 to 3 inches long and often as wide.

FRUIT: What appears to be a berry is actually the seed of the plant; it is round and covered by a thinly fleshy, deep-blue coat with a powdery bloom. Each is about ⅜ inch across; the stemlet is thin and green where it joins the flowering stalk, thickening where it joins the seed to somewhat resemble a tiny blue light bulb. The seeds are generally regarded as toxic, but some sources report that they can be roasted and used as a coffee substitute.

SEASON: Seeds have a greenish coat in early summer; the coat turns blue in mid to late summer.

COMPARE: Although blue cohosh plants don't resemble blueberries at all, care should be taken when in the woods with children, who may mistake the highly visible blue berries of blue cohosh as the edible blueberry. Leaves resemble those of meadow rue (*Thalictrum* spp.), but meadow rue produce dry seed pods, unlike the seed of blue cohosh.

NOTES: Blue cohosh root has been used medicinally to induce labor, and to treat various other gynecological conditions.

green = key identification feature

WOODY
VINE

ALTERNATE
LEAVES

LATE SUMMER
TO FALL

Supplejack –OR– Rattanvine

Berchemia scandens

HABITAT: Moist areas including ravines, thickets, open woods and streambanks; also found in dry, rocky glades and along rocky bluffs.

GROWTH: This native woody vine has no tendrils; it climbs by winding its stems around trees, fences or other supports. Stems are supple and strong; they are green, brown or reddish, often with gray mottling, and have subtle vertical grooves when young. The main stems are dark gray or brown, and may be up to 7 inches across at the base. The stems are very strong and can girdle trees, becoming embedded in the bark as the tree grows. When they grow in moist areas, supplejack vines are longer, up to 50 feet in length; in dry habitat, they tend to be short and tangled.

LEAVES: Egg-shaped to oval leaves grow alternately on ¼- to ½-inch petioles (stemlets); they are 2 to 3½ inches in length and one-half as wide. The veins are numerous, almost straight, parallel and close together; they are raised on the underside. Edges are smooth or finely serrated, and often appear wavy or scalloped; the top side is dark green and glossy. Leaf tips may be rounded or pointy.

FRUIT: Egg-shaped drupes, about ½ inch long and half as wide, grow on thin stalks in clusters at the ends of stems; they are dark blue to bluish-black when ripe. The fruits are bitter and mildly toxic and should not be eaten.

SEASON: Small greenish-yellow flowers appear in mid to late spring; fruits ripen from late summer to fall.

COMPARE: The leaves resemble those of Carolina buckthorn (pg. 170), but Carolina buckthorn is a shrub, not a vine, and its fruits are red.

NOTES: Stems of this plant are used to make wicker furniture, giving the plant its common name of rattanvine. Raccoons, squirrels, and numerous species of birds including quail and wild turkey, enjoy the ripe fruits. Supplejack is considered endangered in Illinois.

green = key identification feature

WOODY
VINE

ALTERNATE
COMPOUND
LEAVES

LATE SUMMER
TO EARLY FALL

Virginia Creeper

Parthenocissus quinquefolia

HABITAT: Moist, well-drained areas including forest edges, cliff bases, streambanks, fence rows, ravines and urban areas. Prefers sun.

GROWTH: A sprawling, native vine that uses sucker-foot tendrils with many branches to attach itself to fences, buildings, walls and other plants, Virginia creeper can grow to 50 feet in length. Older stems at the base of the plant are tan, with rough, shreddy bark; young stems are tan or reddish, with light-colored lenticels (breathing pores).

LEAVES: The palmately compound, shiny leaves typically have five leaflets (occasionally three or seven); they average 7 inches across and grow alternately on long petioles (stemlets) which are often reddish or purplish. Leaflets are oval with tapering ends and a pointed tip; edges above the base are sharply toothed. Generally, two leaflets are much smaller than the others. Leaves are bright green above, paler below; they turn bright scarlet in early fall.

FRUIT: Round berries, about ¼ inch across, grow in loose, open clusters on bright pink stemlets originating opposite a leaf. Berries are deep bluish-purple with a dusty bloom when ripe. According to the USDA and other sources, the berries are highly toxic, while other sources list them as edible but not particularly tasty. It's best to avoid them.

SEASON: Berries ripen in late summer to early fall, and may persist on the plant after the leaves drop in the fall.

COMPARE: Berries resemble wild grapes (pg. 196); the resemblance is unfortunate, because these two plants often grow together. The hot-pink berry stemlets and palmately compound leaves make Virginia creeper easy to identify and avoid. Woodbine (*P. vitacea*) is related, and very similar; however, its tendrils have only a few branches and usually lack sucker-feet, its fruits are slightly larger and its leaves are slightly smaller. Woodbine is much less common in our area.

NOTES: Virginia creeper is the larval host of the Virginia creeper sphinx moth. The berries are eaten by many species of birds.

green = key identification feature

Fall leaf color

TENDER
VINE

ALTERNATE
LEAVES

LATE SUMMER
TO EARLY FALL

Yellow Passionflower

Passiflora lutea

HABITAT: This native vine is found in areas with moist, well-drained soil including open woods, thickets, roadsides and railroad embankments. It prefers sunny areas, but will tolerate partial shade.

GROWTH: A non-woody vine up to 15 feet in length, passionflower uses tendrils to twine itself around other plants, fences and buildings; if a supporting structure is not present, it will sprawl along the ground. Stems are slightly hairy. Distinctive yellowish-green, frilly flowers, ¾ to 1 inch across, grow throughout the summer from leaf axils.

LEAVES: Broad, three-lobed leaves grow alternately from 1½- to 2-inch-long petioles (stemlets). Leaves are generally 2 to 5 inches in width, and about two-thirds as long. The lobes are distinct but fairly shallow, with rounded tips; the central lobe is sometimes longer than the side lobes. The top surface is dull green, occasionally mottled with lighter patches; the underside is paler. Edges are smooth and untoothed.

FRUIT: Round berries, typically ½ to ¾ inch in length, are green when immature, ripening to deep blue with a dusty bloom. Berries grow on long stemlets from leaf axils, and have a thickened collar where they are joined to the stemlet. They are filled with numerous small seeds surrounded by gel-like pulp. The seedy pulp is edible, but the fruits are so small that they are generally not gathered by foragers.

SEASON: Flowers are present from mid to late summer; fruits ripen from late summer through early fall.

COMPARE: Purple passionflower (pg. 50) is a similar vine which grows much more aggressively; it has deeply lobed leaves and larger purple flowers, and its ripe fruits are large and green. Yellow passionflower leaves somewhat resemble those of Canada moonseed (pg. 198), but moonseed has no tendrils; the leaf stalk is attached slightly away from the base of the leaf (peltate).

NOTES: The flowers attract numerous species of butterflies and bees; the berries are eaten by birds and small mammals.

green = key identification feature

Yellow passionflower
climbing in loblolly pine

DELICIOUS

SMALL
WOODY SHRUB

ALTERNATE
LEAVES

MID TO
LATE SUMMER

Blue Ridge

Lowbush

Blue Ridge Blueberry –AND–
Lowbush Blueberry *Vaccinium pallidum, V. angustifolium*

HABITAT: Rocky or gravelly areas on the edges of coniferous and mixed-wood forests; clearings; along footpaths; sunny hilltops and ridges. Blueberries are one of the first plants to appear after a forest fire.

GROWTH: Two types of native low-growing blueberries are found in our area: Blue Ridge blueberry (*Vaccinium pallidum*, sometimes listed as *V. vacillans*) and lowbush blueberry (*V. angustifolium*, sometimes called sweet lowbush blueberry). They are low, sprawling, woody shrubs, up to **3 feet in height**; they often grow in spreading colonies.

LEAVES: Alternate, oval leaves taper on both ends; edges have very fine teeth, and the tip is a slightly rounded point. Leaves are deep green to bluish-green, turning red in fall. Blue Ridge blueberry leaves are 1 to 2 inches in length and about half as wide; those of lowbush blueberries are ½ to 1 inch long and one-third as wide, and are sometimes tinged with red well before fall leaf color appears.

FRUIT: Round berries with a **prominent five-pointed crown** on the bottom; when ripe, they are blue with a **dusty bloom**. Berries are ¼ to ½ inch across, with **small, soft seeds**; they grow in clusters on short stemlets originating in leaf axils. Ripe berries are delicious raw or cooked. Although there are other plants with berries that are blue, there are no toxic look-alikes as long as good identification practices are followed.

SEASON: Berries ripen in mid to late summer.

COMPARE: Two similar shrubs with edible berries may be found in our area. Huckleberries (pg. 268) have ripe fruits that are blackish and less bloomy. Velvet-leaf blueberry (*V. myrtilloides*) is found in our area in a few Iowa and Illinois counties; its leaves are softly hairy beneath. Highbush blueberry (*V. corymbosum*) is a tall shrub with similar leaves and fruits; in our area, it grows only in northeastern Illinois.

NOTES: Lowbush blueberry is listed as threatened in Iowa.

green = key identification feature

Lowbush blueberries

SMALL
WOODY SHRUB

ALTERNATE
LEAVES

LATE
SUMMER

• see below

Common Juniper

Juniperus communis

HABITAT: Dry, sunny openings in mixed-wood and coniferous forests; also found on rocky outcrops, ridges and exposed slopes.

GROWTH: In our area, common juniper is a **sprawling evergreen shrub**, up to 4 feet in height, with short branches that tend to grow upright. It can also grow as a tree, but that form is not generally found in our area. Bark is reddish-brown, fibrous and shreddy. Common juniper is unisexual—a plant is either male or female, and each produces a different type of fruit.

LEAVES: Narrow, pointed, awl-like evergreen needles, about ½ inch in length, grow alternately in clusters of three; they have a strong smell which is both piney and resinous. Needles are **concave on top, with a whitish center**; undersides are dark green. Except near the tip of the branch, needles usually grow almost perpendicular to the branches, giving each branch a bushy appearance.

FRUIT: The female fruit is a round, berry-like cone, about ⅓ inch across, that grows on a short stemlet or is connected directly to the branch. Cones are **bluish-white, with a waxy bloom**; they are usually pro-fuse. When crushed, they **smell like gin**. (The male fruit, a short cat-kin, is borne on separate plants.) The cones are used as a seasoning.

SEASON: Fruits ripen in late summer, and usually persist through winter.

COMPARE: Creeping juniper (*J. horizontalis)* and Ashe's juniper (*J. ashei)* are short shrubs like common juniper, but their leaves are scaly and overlapping, growing very close to the stem. In our area, creeping juniper's range is similar to common juniper's, whereas Ashe's juniper is found only in extreme southwestern Missouri.

NOTES: Common juniper is the most widespread conifer in the world. It is native to the United States and Canada, as well as Eurasia, Japan, Croatia and Sweden; it typically grows as a columnar tree in areas other than North America, although the tree form is found in New England. The cones of common juniper are used to flavor gin.

green = key identification feature   * specific IA locations not available

LARGE WOODY SHRUB

OPPOSITE LEAVES

MID TO LATE SUMMER

Silky

Stiff

Roundleaf

Dogwood (several)

Cornus spp.

HABITAT: Three species of native dogwood with blue fruits and opposite leaves inhabit our region: silky or swamp (*Cornus amomum* and its subspecies, *C. amomum* ssp. *obliqua*), stiff (*C. foemina*), and round-leaf (*C. rugosa*). They are found in mixed forests, and along streams, ponds and lakes; silky and stiff dogwood also grow in low, wet areas.

GROWTH: Broad, open shrubs, typically 6 to 10 feet in height; they spread by suckering and may form colonies. Silky dogwood stems are purplish-red and finely hairy, with brown pith; branches have a smooth green base, overlaid with an open network of brown bark. Stiff dogwood has reddish twigs that turn brown with age; the pith is white. Roundleaf stems are greenish with scattered purple streaks.

LEAVES: Leaves grow oppositely, on medium-length petioles (stemlets); veins curve inward to follow the edge contour. Edges are untoothed, and often appear wavy. Silky and stiff dogwood leaves are oval with a sharp tip, 2 to 4 inches in length and one-half as wide, tapering on both ends. Roundleaf dogwood leaves are broadly egg-shaped, 3 to 6 inches in length and two-thirds as wide; the tip comes to a short, sharp point. Silky and stiff dogwood leaves have three to five pairs of shallow veins per side; roundleaf has six to nine pairs of slightly deeper veins.

FRUIT: Round, smooth drupes, averaging ¼ inch across, grow in flat, loose clusters at branch tips; fruit stemlets are purplish on silky and stiff dogwood, red on roundleaf. When ripe, silky and stiff dogwood fruits are medium to deep blue; roundleaf fruits are paler blue. All are inedible.

SEASON: Fruits ripen in mid to late summer.

COMPARE: Pagoda dogwood (pg. 234) has dark blue fruits on coral-red stemlets, but leaves are alternate or grow in whorls at the ends of branches. Flowering dogwood (pg. 184) has leaves that are similar to silky dogwood, but ripe fruits are red and grow in tight clusters.

NOTES: Roundleaf may also be found occasionally in other parts of Iowa.

green = key identification feature

NOT EDIBLE

Silky dogwood

Silky dogwood branch

Roundleaf dogwood

Roundleaf dogwood stem

LARGE
WOODY SHRUB

OPPOSITE
LEAVES

LATE SUMMER
TO FALL

Southern   Smooth   Softleaf

Arrowwood (several)

Viburnum spp.

HABITAT: Three native arrowwoods with blue fruits are found in our area: southern (*Viburnum dentatum*, pictured at right), smooth (*V. recognitum*, sometimes called northern arrowwood) and softleaf (*V. molle*). They are found along streams, in moist woodlands, and on steep slopes. They grow best in moderate shade to full sun.

GROWTH: Multi-branched shrubs up to 15 feet in height; branches are straight or gently arched. Young stems are brownish, and are sometimes velvety; they may develop slight ridges as they grow. Bark of the main trunk is gray or brown, with pale pores; it becomes loose on softleaf arrowwood and often peels off.

LEAVES: Broadly egg-shaped to almost circular, with sharp, coarse teeth and deeply indented veins. Leaves grow oppositely on a long petiole (stemlet); petioles of softleaf arrowwood have tiny reddish glands (visible with a lens). Top sides are dark green and smooth. Undersides are paler; smooth arrowwood leaves are smooth underneath, while those of southern and softleaf are hairy. Leaves are typically 2 to 4½ inches long, and equally wide; softleaf has a heart-shaped base.

FRUIT: Round to egg-shaped drupes, roughly ¼ inch across, grow in flat, loose clusters at branch tips. The drupes are smooth and opaque, with a slight projection or bump on the bottom; they are blue to bluish-black when ripe. The fruits are bitter and inedible.

SEASON: Flat-topped clusters of white flowers with an unpleasant scent appear from late spring to early summer; the fruits are ripe in late summer to early fall.

COMPARE: Downy arrowwood (pg. 278) is a related plant with similar leaves, but its fruits are black when ripe. Several dogwoods in our area (pgs. 230, 234) have clusters of blue fruits, but their leaves lack the large, coarse teeth found on arrowwood.

NOTES: Softleaf arrowwood is considered endangered in Illinois.

green = key identification feature

LARGE SHRUB
OR SMALL TREE

ALTERNATE
LEAVES

MID TO
LATE SUMMER

Pagoda Dogwood

Cornus alternifolia

HABITAT: Rich, mixed-wood and deciduous forests; rocky slopes; stream and swamp borders. Prefers moderate shade and well-drained soil.

GROWTH: A large native shrub that sometimes appears as a small tree, up to 25 feet tall with a flat-topped, spreading crown. Branches are tiered, with upturned ends; many grow parallel to the ground, giving the shrub a layered appearance. Young stems are greenish or reddish-purple; older bark is grayish-brown, with a rough, often furrowed texture.

LEAVES: Also called alternate-leaf dogwood, pagoda is the only dogwood with alternate leaves, which grow sparsely along the branches. At the ends of the branches, leaves grow in whorled clusters. Leaves are oval, tapering on both ends, with smooth edges, a sharp tip and long petiole (stemlet). Each leaf has five or six pairs of distinct veins that curve in towards the tip; the leaf surface is somewhat pillowy between the veins. Leaves are 2 to 5 inches long and one-half as wide; they are deep green and smooth above, paler and slightly hairy below.

FRUIT: Round, dark blue drupes, ¼ inch across, grow in flat, loose clusters at branch tips. The drupes are smooth and opaque, with a slight whitish bloom; stemlets are bright coral-red. The fruits are inedible.

SEASON: Fruits are greenish when young, gradually becoming reddish or lavender; they ripen fully in mid to late summer.

COMPARE: Three other native dogwoods with blue fruits are found in our area, but their leaves are opposite, not alternate; please see pg. 230 for full descriptions. Arrowwood (pg. 232) also has blue fruits, but it has coarsely toothed leaves that grow oppositely.

NOTES: The fruits fall off or are eaten by wildlife fairly quickly, but the red stemlets remain, making an interesting display.

green = key identification feature

LARGE SHRUB
OR SMALL TREE

OPPOSITE
LEAVES

LATE SUMMER
TO EARLY FALL

Fringetree

Chionanthus virginicus

HABITAT: Areas with moist, well-drained soil, including woodlands, hillsides, limestone glades, rocky ledges and bluffs; also found along creeks and ponds. It prefers sun, but will grow in partial shade.

GROWTH: A large native shrub that sometimes appears as a small tree, fringetree can be up to 35 feet high in the wild; cultivated specimens are typically shorter. It typically has **multiple stems** at the base, and side branches are sometimes crooked, giving the shrub a **gnarly shape**. Young stems are tan or orangish, turning gray and knobby with age. The trunk is brown to gray, with rough ridges. Fringetree is unisexual—a plant is either male or female, and each produces a different type of flower. Those on the male plant are extremely showy, with an abundance of **long, thin white petals** that give the plant its other common name, old man's beard.

LEAVES: Oval leaves with a tapered base and a pointed tip are 4 to 8 inches in length, and one-half to one-third as wide; edges are smooth, and the midvein is prominent. Top sides of mature leaves are dark green and smooth, while the undersides are paler with small hairs on the veins; young leaves are yellowish-green. Leaves grow oppositely on hairy, ½-inch petioles (stemlets); at branch tips, the leaves grow so closely together that they appear **whorled**.

FRUIT: A juicy, egg-shaped drupe, growing in clusters from the branch tips on female plants. The drupes are ½ to ¾ inch long; they are green and speckled when immature, ripening to smooth **bluish-purple with a whitish bloom**. The fruits are inedible.

SEASON: Masses of white flowers appear in late spring; fruits ripen in late summer to early fall.

COMPARE: Immature fruits somewhat resemble Russian olive (pg. 76), but Russian olive's leaves are long and narrow.

NOTES: The fleshy fruits are a valuable food for birds and other wildlife.

green = key identification feature

TREE

OPPOSITE
LEAVES

LATE
SUMMER

Eastern Red Cedar
Juniperus virginiana

HABITAT: Rich, moist mixed-wood forests; abandoned agricultural areas; rocky outcrops and glades; pastures and clearings. Often found in areas with limestone; occasionally found in swampy areas.

GROWTH: This columnar native evergreen tree is usually 40 to 50 feet tall when found in the wild, but can grow to 100 feet. Young twigs are greenish and scaly; branches are brownish-red. The oldest bark is shreddy, peeling off in long strips; exposed wood is gray. Eastern red cedar is generally unisexual—a plant is either male or female, and each produces a different type of fruit. It can be invasive in prairies.

LEAVES: Two types of evergreen leaves grow on eastern red cedar. The primary type are tiny scales, which overlap so tightly on small twigs that the twigs appear to be four-sided, grayish-green scaly leaves. Young trees and new growth have pointed, awl-like needles, which are dark blue-green and about ½ inch long, growing in whorls of three. The foliage has a strong smell which is both piney and resinous.

FRUIT: The female fruit is an oblong, berry-like cone, about ¼ inch across, that grows at the tips of scale-covered branches. Cones are bluish, with a waxy bloom; they are usually profuse. (Male fruits are borne on separate plants; they look like small brown, tightly lapped "pine cones" growing at the ends of branches.) Female cones reportedly can be roasted to use as a coffee substitute, but are not edible.

SEASON: Fruits ripen in late summer, and usually persist through winter.

COMPARE: Creeping juniper (*J. horizontalis*; in our area, found in northeastern Illinois and scattered spots in Iowa) and Ashe's juniper (*J. ashei*; in our area, found only in extreme southwestern Missouri) have scaly leaves like those of eastern red cedar, but they are short, spreading shrubs.

NOTES: Red cedar wood contains an oil that is a natural insect repellent. It is used to line chests (and make pencils), and also chipped for use as bedding for hamsters and other pet rodents.

green = key identification feature

TREE

ALTERNATE
LEAVES

LATE SUMMER
TO FALL

Sassafras

Sassafras albidum

HABITAT: This native tree is found in abandoned fields, open woodlands and forest openings, and along roads and fencerows; it often grows as a pioneer plant on disturbed sites. It produces suckers, and may form dense thickets. Sassafras grows best in sandy soil and partial shade, but will tolerate a range of soil and full sun.

GROWTH: A medium-sized tree, 30 to 60 feet in height, with a broad, rounded crown. Twigs are smooth and yellowish-green; the trunk is reddish-brown and deeply furrowed, with flat-topped ridges. Sassafras trees are unisexual—a tree is either male or female, and each produces a different type of flower.

LEAVES: Three shapes grow on sassafras trees. Some are oval, but the most characteristic leaves have two or three lobes with deep sinuses (the curved depression between the lobes). The lobes are not symmetrical on two-lobed leaves, so the leaf resembles a mitten; three-lobed leaves are fairly symmetrical. Leaves are 3 to 7 inches in length, and about two-thirds as wide; edges are smooth, and the base is sharply tapered. The leaves grow alternately on long, reddish petioles (stemlets); they are bright green above, and white beneath. Trees growing in alkaline soil have yellowish-green leaves with darker areas around the veins. In fall, the leaves turn yellow, orange or scarlet.

FRUIT: Oval, deep-blue drupes, about ½ inch long, grow singly or in clusters on long, curved red stalks at the branch tips of female trees. The top of the stalk, at the base of the fruit, is swollen and cup-like. The fruits are inedible.

SEASON: Fruits mature in late summer to fall.

COMPARE: Mulberries (pg. 172) have some mitten-like leaves, but the leaves are toothy and the fruits are compound drupes.

NOTES: All parts of the plant have a spicy scent, and were used medicinally by American Indians and pioneers. Ground dried leaves are sold as filé, a powder used to thicken gumbo; root bark is used to brew tea.

green = key identification feature

TREE

ALTERNATE
LEAVES

LATE SUMMER
TO FALL

Blackgum –or– Tupelo

Nyssa sylvatica

HABITAT: This native tree grows in areas with rich, moist soil. It is found next to streams and ponds, in swampy areas and creek bottoms, and in openings in damp woodlands. It prefers full sun, and is tolerant of seasonal flooding.

GROWTH: A medium to large tree, often 60 to 80 feet in height, with dense foliage and a pyramidal crown. The trunk, which may be up to 3 feet thick, is straight, and branches are horizontal or slightly drooping. Branches are smooth and gray or reddish, with small lenticels (breathing pores); the trunk is dark grayish-brown, with irregular, flat ridges.

LEAVES: Glossy, leathery oval leaves, 4 to 6 inches in length and one-half as wide, grow alternately on short petioles (stemlets); leaves often cluster on short spur branches along the main branch. They are deep green on top, yellowish-green underneath. Edges are smooth, but some leaves have several very large teeth that look like pointed lobes. Leaf bases may be rounded or tapered; tips come to a blunt point. The leaves turn brilliant scarlet, orange or purplish in fall.

FRUIT: Round to oval drupes, about ½ inch long, grow singly or in small clusters on long, thin stemlets along side branches; ripe fruits are dark blue with a dusty bloom. They contain a single, large pit; the flesh is thin but juicy, with a bitter flavor reminiscent of lime peels. The fruits can be eaten in the field as an astringent refresher; according to some reports, they can also be used to make preserves.

SEASON: Fruits ripen in late summer to fall.

COMPARE: The related swamp tupelo (*N. biflora*) is very similar, but its leaves are 2 to 4 inches in length and about one-third as wide; it grows only in swampy areas. Persimmon (pg. 88) has similar leaves and patchy bark, but its fruits are large, globe-shaped berries with a sturdy crown-like cap; its leaves are dull rather than shiny, and do not turn red in fall.

NOTES: Birds devour the fruit very quickly upon its ripening. Honey made by bees feeding on tupelo is very highly regarded.

green = key identification feature

TENDER
LEAFY PLANT

SINGLE
COMPOUND
LEAF

SUMMER

Sarsaparilla

Aralia nudicaulis

HABITAT: Rich, moist, sun-dappled mixed-wood and hardwood forests; thickets and prairie areas; occasionally near streams and bogs.

GROWTH: This native plant has a single, three-stemmed, doubly compound leaf growing from the underground rhizome (root-bearing stem) at the top of a long, erect hairless leaf stalk; total height may be as much as 2 feet, but it is usually shorter. The flowering/fruiting stalk is separate, rising from the same point as the leaf stalk; it is shorter, typically 5 to 8 inches in height.

LEAVES: Three-part, doubly compound; each of the three leaf stalks has three to five oblong, toothy leaflets with rounded bases and pointed tips. Leaflets are 2 to 4 inches long and about two-thirds as wide; they are broadest at or below the midpoint.

FRUIT: The leafless fruiting stalk divides into three stemlets (occasionally two); each is topped with a rounded cluster of black berries on slender stemlets that emanate from a central point, much like the fluffy head of a dandelion gone to seed. Berries are round, and about ⅛ inch in diameter. They are inedible when raw; although they may be edible when cooked, sources disagree on this, so they are best left to the birds, foxes and bears, who consume them with no ill effects.

SEASON: Fruits ripen in midsummer.

COMPARE: With its distinctive three-part, doubly compound leaf, and separate, fruiting stalk topped with ball-shaped berry clusters, sarsaparilla really doesn't resemble anything else in the woods.

NOTES: The underground rhizome is very fragrant, and has been used to make tea and other beverages. It is not, however, the source of the flavoring in root beer and the soft drink called sarsaparilla; rather, that flavor traditionally came from the roots and bark of the unrelated sassafras tree (pg. 240).

green = key identification feature

TENDER
LEAFY PLANT

ALTERNATE
LEAVES

LATE
SUMMER

American Pokeweed
Phytolacca americana

HABITAT: Agricultural areas, waste ground, fencelines, railroad beds, field edges, shelterbelts, disturbed sites. Requires adequate moisture; can grow in sun or shade.

GROWTH: An upright, multi-branching native leafy plant, up to 12 feet in height but generally much shorter. Stems are green when young, turning reddish or purplish as they mature. The central stem often becomes quite thick, up to 1 inch in diameter.

LEAVES: Alternate, oblong leaves, up to 12 inches long and roughly one-third as wide. The base of leaf tapers into the long petiole (stemlet); the leaf is broadest at the midpoint, tapering to a point at the tip. Leaves are bright green and coarsely textured with smooth edges; they have an unpleasant scent when crushed.

FRUIT: The most distinctive part of the plant. Shiny, purplish-black berries with an indent in the bottom, each ¼ to ⅓ inch wide and often slightly flattened, grow in a raceme (a long fruit cluster) from hot-pink stemlets; the hanging fruit stem is also hot pink, and up to 15 inches in length. The berries are poisonous, containing toxic alkaloids.

SEASON: Berries develop in early to mid summer; they are green at first, turning white with white stemlets, before ripening in late summer.

COMPARE: When it is fruiting, pokeweed is hard to miss, or to confuse with other plants. The dark berries on the hot-pink stem, combined with the overall size of the plant and its leaves, make this plant easy to identify.

NOTES: Although *all parts of the pokeweed plant contain deadly, toxic alkaloids*, young shoots of pokeweed are traditionally eaten as a cooked green, especially in the South; special preparations are needed to eliminate the toxic constituents. Sap from the plant can cause an allergic reaction in sensitive individuals. The berries can be used to produce ink and a red dye; according to some sources, the juice was used in the past to intensify the color of cheap wine.

green = key identification feature

TENDER
LEAFY PLANT

ALTERNATE
LEAVES

MIDSUMMER
TO EARLY FALL

Eastern Black Nightshade   *Solanum ptycanthum*

HABITAT: Agricultural areas, waste ground, urban areas, thickets, wood-land openings, rocky ground and vacant lots. It does best in partial to full sun, and can adapt to moist or dry conditions.

GROWTH: A tender, branching native perennial, up to 3 feet in height but often shorter. Young stems are green and round, often with scattered hairs; they become brownish, angular and woody over the season.

LEAVES: Alternate, slightly hairy on both surfaces. Purplish when young changing to deep green, although undersides are typically tinged with purple even on mature leaves. The shape is inconsistent; in general, they are broadly triangular to elliptic, but edges may be smooth and wavy, or may have wide, blunt teeth. Larger leaves are up to 3 inches in length and two-thirds as wide, although the plant typically has numerous smaller leaves near the ends of the branches.

FRUIT: Round berries, about ⅓ inch in diameter with a star-shaped cap, grow in hanging clusters of five to seven. Berries are hard and green when young, softening and ripening to a deep, glossy black; they have juicy pulp and numerous flat seeds. Underripe berries are toxic. Some foragers eat fully ripe berries in small quantities, but even this may cause intestinal problems in some people. For more information on judging ripeness and eating berries, consult *Nature's Garden* (Sam Thayer). To avoid potential problems, simply consider them inedible.

SEASON: Small, white, star-shaped flowers grow throughout summer; berries follow, ripening throughout midsummer and into early fall.

COMPARE: Climbing nightshade (pg. 120) grows as a vine; its fruits are red when ripe. Two other non-vining nightshades occasionally grow in our area. Berries of cutleaf nightshade (*S. triflorum*) are orange when ripe; those of hoe nightshade (*S. physalifolium*) are yellowish-green.

NOTES: Sometimes listed as a synonym for black nightshade (*S. nigrum*); however, according to the USDA PLANTS database, *S. nigrum* is a separate species that grows on both coasts and in Canada, but not here.

green = key identification feature

TENDER OR
WOODY VINE

ALTERNATE
LEAVES

MID TO LATE
SUMMER

* see below

Smilax (several)

Smilax spp.

HABITAT: These native vines grow in openings in moist, rich deciduous forests; also streambanks, thickets, clearings, waste ground.

GROWTH: *Smilax* is a family of vines, up to 10 feet in length. Some use tendrils to climb over other plants, while others lack tendrils, reclining over other plants when they become too tall to support themselves. There are two types of *Smilax*: non-woody (also called carrion-flower) and woody (also called greenbrier). In our area, non-woody species include common *Smilax* (*Smilax lasioneura*), upright (*S. ecirrhata*), smooth (*S. herbacea*), Illinois (*S. illinoensis*), and downy (*S. pulverulenta*). Woody species include catbrier (*S. rotundifolia*), saw greenbrier (*S. bona-nox*), whiteleaf greenbrier (*S. glauca*), and bristly greenbrier (*S. tamnoides*). Woody species have bristles and, sometimes, thorns.

LEAVES: Most *Smilax* in our area have broadly oval or heart-shaped leaves, with several deep parallel veins that have a web of smaller veins between them. Saw greenbrier leaves, however, have three rounded lobes that lack the web of veins; leaf edges are spiny. Leaves of all *Smilax* grow alternately along the stem; they are generally 3 to 5 inches long and one-half to three-quarters as wide. Most are dark green on top, paler underneath; whiteleaf greenbrier are white underneath, and saw greenbrier may have light splotches on top.

FRUIT: Both woody and non-woody *Smilax* produce similar rounded or ball-shaped clusters of berries on long, stiff stalks. Ripe fruits of all *Smilax* in our area are bluish-black with a whitish bloom. The fruits are generally considered edible, but are not very tasty.

SEASON: Berries ripen in mid to late summer, and may persist into winter.

COMPARE: The berry cluster may sometimes be mistaken for wild grapes (pg. 196); however, the stalk on *Smilax* makes identification easy.

NOTES: For information that helps identify most of the *Smilax* in our area, please visit the website of the Robert W. Freckmann Herbarium (University of Wisconsin, Stevens Point) at http://wisplants.uwsp.edu.

green = key identification feature   * combined range

Common carrion-flower

Lower stem of
bristly greenbrier

WOODY
VINE

ALTERNATE
COMPOUND
LEAVES

LATE SUMMER
TO FALL

Amur Peppervine

Ampelopsis arborea

HABITAT: Wet areas, including marshes, floodplains, swamps, stream and river banks, abandoned fields, road ditches and low thickets. It produces abundant fruit in full sun, less in shady areas.

GROWTH: This native vine often sprawls along the ground like a ground-cover, but is more often a high-climbing vine. It can grow to 35 feet in length; it is typically a very full, bushy plant, whether reclining or climbing. Young stems are reddish and often have fine hairs; older stems are brownish and woody, with warty lenticels (breathing pores). It has occasional tendrils opposite the leaves.

LEAVES: Twice- or thrice-divided compound leaves grow alternately. Each leaf is 3 to 7 inches in length and width; the leaf stalk is reddish, and grooved on one side. Two to six compound leaflets grow from each leaf stalk; a terminal three-part compound leaflet is also present. Individual leaflets are up to 1½ inches long and about two-thirds as wide, with very coarse teeth; they are dark green and smooth above, lighter green below with scattered hairs on the veins. Young leaves are reddish and very shiny. The foliage turns yellowish or red in fall.

FRUIT: Round or slightly flattened berries, ¼ to ⅜ inch across, grow in loose clusters on leafless stemlets. Berries are pale when young, turning bright red before ripening to shiny black. Some sources list the fruit as edible, but most reliable sources say that edibility is questionable and the flavor poor. It is best to treat them as inedible.

SEASON: Berries are ripe from late summer to fall.

COMPARE: Fruits may resemble grapes (pg. 196), but grapes do not have compound leaves. The leaves are similar to those of trumpet creeper (*Campsis radicans*), a native vine found throughout much of Missouri and Illinois; however, trumpet creeper's fruits are long pods.

NOTES: Amur peppervine grows vigorously and spreads aggressively, and is considered a nuisance plant in some areas. Small mammals eat the fruits; deer occasionally browse on the leaves.

green = key identification feature

WOODY
VINE

ALTERNATE
LEAVES

LATE SUMMER
TO FALL

Cupseed

Calycocarpum lyonii

HABITAT: Areas with rich, moist soil including streambanks, floodplain forests, river bottoms, valleys and field edges.

GROWTH: A native woody vine, up to 30 feet in length, that climbs by twining itself around fences, trees and other plants; it has no tendrils. It may die back to the ground in winter; new growth is tender and green, so the vine may appear non-woody. Stems are smooth and yellowish-brown to gray, with fine grooves and dark speckles.

LEAVES: Alternate, on petioles (stemlets) that are up to 6 inches in length. Leaves may be palmately lobed, or heart-shaped (unlobed). The lobed leaves, 3 to 8 inches long and almost as wide, have three to five lobes with pointed tips; the sinuses (depressions between the lobes) are deep around the central lobe, shallower between the other lobes (when present). Unlobed leaves are typically 3 to 6 inches in length and almost as wide; they are broadest at the base, and may have scattered large teeth. The upper sides of all leaves are smooth and bright green; undersides are slightly paler, with scattered hairs on the veins.

FRUIT: Fleshy, globe-shaped or oval drupes grow in tight, hanging clusters on long stemlets opposite a leaf. The fruits are ¾ to 1 inch long, and greenish-blackish when ripe, with no bloom; each contains a single seed shaped like a shallow cup. The fruits are inedible.

SEASON: Fruits are ripe in late summer to fall.

COMPARE: Cupseed's fruit clusters are 2 to 3 inches long and bear a resemblance to grapes (pg. 196); the leaves are similar to some grape species. Grapes have tendrils, which are absent on cupseed; grape seeds are not cup-shaped. Care is needed when picking grapes in areas where cupseed is also present. Cupseed's leaves also resemble those of Guadeloupe cucumber (*Melothria pendula*), a native vine that in found in our area in southern Missouri, but Guadeloupe cucumber's leaves are smaller and its fruit resembles a tiny cucumber.

NOTES: Cupseed is a member of the moonseed (pg. 198) family.

green = key identification feature

Unripe fruit

WOODY
VINE

OPPOSITE
LEAVES

LATE SUMMER
TO FALL

Japanese Honeysuckle
Lonicera japonica

HABITAT: This non-native vine has escaped from cultivation, and is increasingly found in a wide variety of habitats including agricultural areas, thickets, woodlands, disturbed areas and alongside roads and railroads. It tolerates shade, but also grows in sunny areas.

GROWTH: A trailing or climbing vine, typically less than 10 feet in length but sometimes longer; it grows compactly and so profusely that it often resembles a shrub from a distance. It has no tendrils, and climbs by twining itself around poles, fences, trees and other plants; it can girdle and kill trees with its twining stems. It often forms dense canopies in forested areas. Young stems are reddish-brown and hairy; older stems and the trunk are tan, with shreddy bark.

LEAVES: Oval leaves, 1 to 3 inches in length and one-half to two-thirds as wide, grow oppositely on short petioles (stemlets). Leaf bases are broad; the tip is often pointed, but may also be rounded. Top sides are bright green, often with fine hairs but sometimes almost smooth; undersides are paler, with hairs along the main vein. Leaves remain green and on the plant until the temperatures drop well below freezing; in protected areas, they may remain through winter.

FRUIT: Round to oval berries, about ¼ inch long, grow singly or in pairs on stubby stalks from leaf axils. Berries are juicy, and contain two or more small seeds; they are glossy black when ripe. They are inedible.

SEASON: Fragrant whitish flowers are present in late spring, turning yellow with age. Berries follow, ripening to black in late summer to fall.

COMPARE: Several native honeysuckle vines grow in our area, but ripe fruits are red, and the leaves at the tip of the stem fuse to form a cup; please see pg. 122 for more information.

NOTES: Japanese honeysuckle is native to Asia; it was brought to this country in the early 1800s as an ornamental and for erosion control. It is considered a noxious, invasive plant due to its rapid, dense growth, which often shades out native plants.

green = key identification feature

SMALL
WOODY SHRUB

ALTERNATE
COMPOUND
LEAVES

SUMMER

Black Raspberry

Rubus occidentalis

HABITAT: Disturbed areas, especially those that have been logged or cut. Also found in tangled meadows, along streams and lakes, next to trails or roads, and in open woods. This native plant grows in both shady and sunny areas, but produces more fruit in moderate to full sun.

GROWTH: Black raspberries are brambles, sprawling vine-like shrubs that often form a thicket. Stems, called canes, grow to 6 feet in length, and usually arch but may also be upright. Black raspberry canes have sharp, curved thorns. Young canes are unbranched and have a whitish bloom that can be rubbed off; older canes are branched and purplish.

LEAVES: Compound, doubly toothed leaves with sharply pointed tips grow alternately on the canes. Leaves usually have three leaflets, occasionally five; they are up to 3 inches long. The terminal leaflet has a long petiole (stemlet); side leaflets attach directly to the stem.

FRUIT: A compound drupe, up to ½ inch across. Fruits are green and hard at first, progressing through several color changes and becoming yellowish, salmon-colored, bright red, purplish-red, and finally ripening to purplish-black. Ripe fruits detach cleanly from the plant, leaving the receptacle (core) behind; the picked fruit is hollow. Fruits are edible and delicious. When the fruits are ripe, there are no toxic look-alikes.

SEASON: Black raspberries ripen in early to midsummer, generally before red raspberries (pg. 130) and well before blackberries (pg. 270).

COMPARE: Red raspberries look similar to underripe black raspberries; however, red raspberry canes are prickly but not thorny and lack the whitish bloom. If you find a raspberry that is red but is still hard and won't detach from the receptacle (core) easily, you've found underripe black raspberries; return in a week to harvest ripe fruit. Blackberries have similar growth habits and a compound fruit that is black at maturity, but the receptacle (core) stays with the berry when it's picked.

NOTES: Black raspberries are considered by many to be the tastiest berry in the *Rubus* family (which includes raspberries and blackberries).

green = key identification feature

SMALL
WOODY SHRUB

ALTERNATE
COMPOUND
LEAVES

SUMMER

Southern

Swamp

Southern Dewberry –AND–
Swamp Dewberry

Rubus trivialis, R. hispidus

HABITAT: Seven varieties of native bristly black dewberry may be found in our area. Only two, southern (*Rubus trivialis*) and swamp (*R. hispidus*), occur with any frequency; the others are found in a few counties per state (or not at all in a particular state). Dewberries grow in rich forests and thickets, along streams, and occasionally in rocky areas.

GROWTH: A trailing, low-growing shrub that may appear vine-like. Stems are woody but weak, usually sprawling along the ground rather than rising erect. They are well armed with extremely sharp, thin bristles. Southern dewberry stems are greenish or brownish, and bear sharp, curved red-tinged thorns in addition to the prickles. Stems of swamp dewberry are usually reddish and without thorns.

LEAVES: Compound, doubly toothy leaves with sharply pointed tips grow alternately on the canes, on long, bristly stems. Leaves of fruiting canes have three leaflets, while those of non-fruiting canes typically have five. The terminal leaflet has a noticeable petiole (stemlet); side leaflets are attached directly to the stem.

FRUIT: The compound drupe, ¼ to ½ inch across, resembles a small blackberry; unlike blackberries, the ripe fruit detaches cleanly (but not easily) from the receptacle (core) so it is hollow when picked. Bristly dewberry fruits are green and hard at first, turning red before ripening to glossy black. Fruits are edible and usually tasty; quality varies from plant to plant. When dewberries are ripe, there are no toxic look-alikes.

SEASON: Dewberries ripen from early to late summer, depending on location and species.

COMPARE: Several non-bristly dewberries grow in our area, and are similar in growth form but lack bristles. Fruits of dwarf raspberry (pg. 118) are red when ripe; smooth black dewberries (pg. 272) are black when ripe.

NOTES: Caution: the thin bristles break off easily and lodge in the skin.

green = key identification feature

Swamp dewberry

SMALL
WOODY SHRUB

ALTERNATE
LEAVES

MID TO
LATE SUMMER

Sand Cherry

Prunus pumila

HABITAT: Open dunes; sandy or gravelly shorelines of lakes and rivers; sandy or rocky edges of coniferous forests; grassy prairie areas. Sand cherry prefers sunny areas and tolerates dry conditions; it can survive harsh winters.

GROWTH: A sparse, low native shrub, 2 to 9 feet in height, with upright branches. In windy areas, it may recline rather than stand upright. Twigs are reddish; branches are reddish-brown, becoming gray with age. Bark is marked with light-colored lenticels (breathing pores).

LEAVES: Narrowly oval, tapering on both ends, with a leathery texture; they grow alternately from the stems on petioles (stemlets) that are often reddish. Leaves are 1 to 2 inches in length and roughly one-third as wide; edges have scattered small teeth, especially toward the tip. Deep green and glossy on top, lighter beneath; tips and leaf edges sometimes have a reddish tinge.

FRUIT: An oval drupe with a single pit; it is about 1 inch long and glossy black when ripe. There is more flesh in proportion to the pit than on chokecherries (pg. 154) or pin cherries (pg. 178). Fruits are edible; they are sweet but somewhat astringent. They are usually cooked to make jam or preserves. There are no toxic look-alikes.

SEASON: Fruits ripen from mid to late summer.

COMPARE: Mexican plum (pg. 212) has a similar fruit, but it is purple when ripe, not black; Mexican plum is a small tree rather than a shrub.

NOTES: The deep roots of sand cherry help stabilize sand dunes around the Great Lakes. The fruit is eaten by large birds; the twigs are browsed by deer and small mammals. Birds use the shrubs for nesting and escape cover. Sand cherry leaves, stems and pits contain hydrocyanic acid, a cyanide-producing compound. The leaves and pits should never be eaten, and care should be taken to avoid crushing the pits when juicing the fruits. Cooking, drying or freezing eliminates the acid.

green = key identification feature

SMALL
WOODY SHRUB

ALTERNATE
LEAVES

MID TO
LATE SUMMER

Missouri Gooseberry

Ribes missouriense

HABITAT: Open woodlands, field borders, clearings, meadows, thickets, and abandoned fields.

GROWTH: An arching native shrub up to 4 feet high. Mature stems typically have scattered thin bristles; smaller stems are usually smooth. Leaf nodes have one to three long thorns that are up to ½ inch long.

LEAVES: Attached alternately to the stem by a long petiole (stemlet); each leaf node has one to three leaves. Each leaf has three to five distinct lobes, resembling a maple leaf with rounded teeth. Leaves are slightly hairy underneath.

FRUIT: The smooth, ¼- to ½-inch round berry grows on a thin stemlet from leaf nodes, singly or in clusters of two or three. Distinct stripes run longitudinally on the berry; a prominent flower remnant, often called a pigtail, is present at the end of the berry. Missouri gooseberries are green when young, maturing to deep purplish-black when ripe. Gooseberries are edible in both the green and ripe stages.

SEASON: Ripe fruits are present from midsummer in the southern part of our region, into late summer in the northern part.

COMPARE: Two other native gooseberries inhabit our region. Stems of prickly gooseberry (pg. 136) have scattered small bristles; those of smooth gooseberry (pg. 202) are smooth or slightly hairy. Ripe fruits of prickly gooseberry are reddish-purple and bear small, soft prickles. Smooth gooseberry are purplish-black, with smooth skins. Currant shrubs (pgs. 134, 266) resemble gooseberry shrubs, but the berries are typically borne in racemes (long clusters of multiple fruits).

NOTES: Ripe gooseberries are excellent in baked desserts, sauces and other dishes. Green gooseberries (pg. 54) are rich in pectin, and are used primarily for jam and jelly.

green = key identification feature

Large thorns

SMALL
WOODY SHRUB

ALTERNATE
LEAVES

MID TO
LATE SUMMER

American

Golden

Black Currant (several)

Ribes spp.

HABITAT: Three varieties of native black currant inhabit our region: American black currant (*Ribes americanum*, pictured at right), golden currant (*R. aureum*, sometimes listed as *R. odoratum*) and northern black currant (*R. hudsonianum*; in our area, found only in a few counties in northeastern Iowa, where it is classified as threatened). All inhabit moist woodlands, swampy areas, thickets and stream banks; golden currant prefers rocky areas.

GROWTH: A straggling shrub, generally 3 to 6 feet in height, that often clambers over other plants; golden currant can reach 9 feet in height. All currants listed here have smooth stems and are thornless.

LEAVES: Attached alternately to the stem by a thin petiole (stemlet). Each leaf has three to five distinct lobes, resembling a maple leaf with rounded teeth. Leaves of American black currant have tiny resin dots on both surfaces (visible with a lens); those of northern black currant have resin dots on the underside only. Leaves of golden currant have no resin dots. When crushed, northern black currant leaves emit an unpleasant odor.

FRUIT: Round ¼- to ⅜-inch berries grow in a raceme (a long cluster of multiple fruits). Immature berries are green, turning red before ripening to black. Berries of northern black currant are smooth but covered in resin dots; they are unpalatable but can be eaten safely. Berries of the other currants listed here are delicious, and can be eaten raw, used in baking, or cooked into jelly, jam and other dishes. There are no toxic look-alikes.

SEASON: Black currants ripen in mid to late summer.

COMPARE: Gooseberries (pgs. 54, 136, 202 and 264) and red currants (pg. 134) have similar leaves and growth habits, but all gooseberries have thorns at the leaf nodes. Gooseberry fruits grow in clusters of two or three, in contrast to currants, which grow in a raceme.

NOTES: Golden currant, also called clove currant, has a clove-like odor.

green = key identification feature

American black currant

SMALL
WOODY SHRUB

ALTERNATE
LEAVES

MID TO
LATE SUMMER

Black Huckleberry

Gaylussacia baccata

HABITAT: Dry habitat, including rocky or sandy areas, open mixed-wood forests, thickets. Sometimes seen growing in thin soil that fills cracks in granite slabs, as in the photo at right.

GROWTH: A low, upright, multi-stemmed native shrub, up to 3 feet in height but usually shorter; often grows in colonies. Branches are greenish or reddish; older stems are gray.

LEAVES: Alternate, roughly oval, tapering at both ends; dark green on top, slightly lighter beneath, with tiny golden resin dots on both surfaces (visible with a lens). Small reddish-purple spots are often present. Leaves are 1 to 3 inches long and one-third to one-half as wide; edges are smooth. They grow on a very short petiole (stemlet).

FRUIT: A round berry has a prominent five-pointed crown on the bottom; when ripe, it is blackish-blue with a dusty bloom. Berries are typically ¼ to ½ inch across, and have greenish flesh with 10 small seeds that are soft but usually noticeable. They grow in short racemes (clusters of multiple fruits) originating in the leaf axils. Ripe huckleberries are delicious raw or cooked. There are no toxic look-alikes.

SEASON: Berries ripen in mid to late summer.

COMPARE: Huckleberries may be mistaken for lowbush blueberries (pg. 226); however, ripe blueberries are blue with a whitish bloom, and their leaves lack the resin dots found on huckleberry leaves. Blueberries are edible and delicious; their seeds are smaller and softer than those of the huckleberry. A taller huckleberry, known variously as blue huckleberry, tall huckleberry or dangleberry (*G. frondosa*) is very similar to black huckleberry, but it can grow up to 6 feet in height. It is a more eastern species that does not grow in our area.

NOTES: Huckleberries and blueberries often grow in the same places. Distinguishing between the two is more a matter of curiosity than of necessity, because they can be used in exactly the same manner as one another. Huckleberry is listed as threatened in Iowa.

green = key identification feature

Unripe berries

SMALL
WOODY SHRUB

ALTERNATE
COMPOUND
LEAVES

MID TO
LATE SUMMER

* see below

Common Blackberry   *Rubus allegheniensis* and others

HABITAT: Scrubby areas, waste ground, pastures, sun-dappled woods, forest clearings and thickets; also found alongside paths and roads.

GROWTH: Blackberries are brambles, sprawling vine-like shrubs that may form a thicket. Stems, called canes, grow to 8 feet in length, and are usually arching but may be upright. Blackberry canes are ridged, and star-shaped in cross-section, with numerous sharp thorns that are often curved. Young canes are reddish or greenish, with no whitish bloom; older canes are brownish. A dozen blackberry varieties grow in our area; several are introduced, but most are native. Some have fewer thorns; they may have smaller leaves or longer fruit clusters, and the depth of the teeth on the leaves varies. All produce edible fruit; exact identification is a matter for botanists.

LEAVES: Compound, doubly toothy, coarsely textured leaves with sharply pointed tips and long stems are attached alternately to the canes; undersides are pale. Leaves of fruiting canes have three leaflets, while those of non-fruiting canes typically have five. Leaves are typically up to 5 inches long; the terminal leaflet is larger than side leaflets.

FRUIT: A compound drupe, about ½ inch across and usually somewhat longer. Fruits are green and hard at first, turning red before ripening to glossy black. The receptacle (core) remains inside the picked berry so the fruit is solid, not hollow like a raspberry. Blackberries are edible raw or cooked; when ripe, there are no toxic look-alikes.

SEASON: Blackberries are red and underripe in early summer; they ripen in mid to late summer, well after red raspberries (pg. 130) and black raspberries (pg. 258).

COMPARE: Several other *Rubus* in our area have black compound drupes. Black raspberries (pg. 258) are hollow when picked; stems have a whitish bloom. Dewberries (pgs. 118, 260 and 272) are trailing rather than arching shrubs; fruits are hollow when picked.

NOTES: Blackberries have larger, coarser seeds than other brambles.

green = key identification feature   * combined range; specific MO locations not available

SMALL
WOODY SHRUB

ALTERNATE
COMPOUND
LEAVES

MID TO
LATE SUMMER

* see below

Common Dewberry

Rubus flagellaris and others

HABITAT: Seven varieties of native non-bristly black dewberry may be found in our region. Only one, common or smooth dewberry (*Rubus flagellaris*), occurs with any frequency; the others are found in only a few counties per state (or not at all in a particular state). Dewberries are found in open forests, thickets, and along streambanks and roads.

GROWTH: A trailing, low-growing shrub that may appear vine-like. Stems are woody but weak, usually sprawling along the ground rather than rising erect; the tips often develop roots. They have curved thorns but no bristles. Northern dewberry stems are greenish or reddish, and sometimes appear angled; they usually have scattered small hairs.

LEAVES: Compound, doubly toothy leaves with sharply pointed tips grow alternately on the canes, on long stems that are usually hairy or prickly. Leaves of fruiting canes have three leaflets, while those of non-fruiting canes typically have five. Leaflets are up to 3 inches in length and two-thirds as wide. The terminal leaflet has a short petiole (stemlet); side leaflets are attached directly to the stem.

FRUIT: The compound drupe, ¼ to ½ inch across, resembles a small black-berry; unlike blackberries, the ripe fruit detaches cleanly (but not eas-ily) from the receptacle (core) so it is hollow when picked. Dewberry fruits are green and hard at first, turning red before ripening to glossy black. Fruits are edible and usually quite tasty; quality varies from plant to plant. When dewberry is ripe, there are no toxic look-alikes.

SEASON: Dewberries ripen from mid to late summer, depending on loca-tion and species.

COMPARE: Several other dewberries grow in our area, and are similar in growth form. Fruits of dwarf raspberry (pg. 118) are red when ripe. Southern and swamp dewberries (pg. 260) are black when ripe, but the plants are armed with thin, sharp bristles.

NOTES: Dewberries grow low to the ground, often between other plants. At a quick glance, the leaves resemble those of wild strawberries.

green = key identification feature   * combined range; specific IA locations not available

SMALL
WOODY SHRUB

ALTERNATE
LEAVES

LATE SUMMER
TO EARLY FALL

Alder-Leaved Buckthorn
Rhamnus alnifolia

HABITAT: Moist areas, including mixed-wood forests, damp meadows, swampy areas, stream banks and thickets. Sometimes found growing on the wet edge of a pond or lake.

GROWTH: A short, upright shrub, 3 feet or less in height and equal spread. Branches fork several times. Twigs are smooth and reddish or brownish; young branches are downy. It may form colonies, with many short shrubs in a tight group. Alder-leaved buckthorn is usually unisexual—a plant is either male or female, and each produces a different type of flower.

LEAVES: Roughly oval, with a sharp tip; each has six to eight pairs of deep, gently curving veins. Leaves are up to 4 inches in length and one-half as wide; they grow alternately from the stems on short, smooth petioles (stemlets). Edges are finely toothed; both surfaces are smooth and somewhat glossy, although the veins may be slightly hairy on the underside. Tiny paired, leaf-like appendages called stipules grow at the base of each leaf petiole.

FRUIT: Glossy round drupes, about ¼ inch in diameter, are red when underripe, turning black when ripe. Fruits grow on thin stemlets from the leaf axils. They are inedible.

SEASON: Fruits are red in late summer, turning black by early fall.

COMPARE: Lanceleaf buckthorn (pg. 276) is much taller, and is found in drier habitat; its leaves are longer, and are generally narrower in proportion to their length than those of alder-leaved buckthorn. Common buckthorn (pg. 280) is another taller shrub found in drier habitat; its leaves are more egg-shaped. Glossy buckthorn (pg. 290) is also taller; it has smooth-edged leaves, and leaf undersides are hairy.

NOTES: Unlike common buckthorn and glossy buckthorn, alder-leaved buckthorn is a native plant; it is not considered invasive, and can sometimes be hard to find.

green = key identification feature

LARGE
WOODY SHRUB

ALTERNATE
LEAVES

MID TO
LATE SUMMER

Lanceleaf Buckthorn

Rhamnus lanceolata

HABITAT: This native shrub is found in areas with a limestone base, including glades, brushy thickets, and open wooded slopes. It prefers moist areas, and may be found near bogs and swamps, but it also tolerates drier soil. It does best in areas with partial shade.

GROWTH: Generally a medium to large shrub, up to 15 feet in height, although it can be much shorter in some locations, remaining under 6 feet. Twigs are slender and greenish to reddish with fine hairs; branches are gray. The trunk is gray; bark of older specimens may peel off in vertical strips.

LEAVES: Oval to almost lance-shaped leaves are up to 5 inches in length and one-third as wide; the tip is softly pointed and the leaf base is tapered. Edges are finely toothed, and may appear slightly wavy; the top surface is deep green and smooth, while the underside is yellowish-green with scattered hairs on the midrib. Leaves grow alternately on ½-inch petioles (stemlets) that are slightly grooved and have fine hairs along the edge; leaves tend to bunch slightly at the branch tips, appearing almost opposite.

FRUIT: Round drupes, about ¼ inch across, grow in clusters on thin stemlets originating in the leaf axils. Fruits are green at first, turning red before ripening to glossy black. The fruits are inedible.

SEASON: Greenish-yellow flowers appear in late spring to early summer; fruits follow, and are ripe in mid to late summer.

COMPARE: Alder-leaved buckthorn (pg. 274) is a related native shrub that is much shorter, usually 3 feet or less, with leaves that are up to 4 inches in length. Carolina buckthorn (pg. 170) is a large shrub with narrow leaves similar to lanceleaf buckthorn, but its fruits are red when ripe. Common buckthorn (pg. 280) is a large shrub with black fruits and similar growth habit, but its leaves are wide and egg-shaped.

NOTES: Lanceleaf buckthorn provides food and shelter for wild birds.

green = key identification feature

Unripe fruit

Ripe fruit

LARGE
WOODY SHRUB

OPPOSITE
LEAVES

LATE
SUMMER

Downy Arrowwood

Viburnum rafinesquianum

HABITAT: Dry mixed-wood and hardwood forests; along streams. Downy arrowwood is drought-tolerant, and very adaptable.

GROWTH: An open, multi-branched native shrub with a rounded top, generally 6 to 8 feet in height and slightly less wide. Branches are erect and straight, spreading outward from the base. The bark is smooth and dark gray; unlike other *Viburnums*, the bark does not become flaky with age.

LEAVES: Opposite, dark green leaves with 10 or fewer pairs of large teeth grow on short, hairy, grooved petioles (stemlets); leaves are 1½ to 3 inches in length and roughly one-third as wide. Leaves are broadest below the midpoint, with a rounded base; they taper to the pointed tip. Leaf edges have very fine hairs (visible with a lens); undersides are densely hairy (particularly on the veins) and light green. Foliage turns rosy maroon in the fall.

FRUIT: Oval to round drupes, each about ⅓ inch long, grow in open, flat-topped clusters at the ends of branches; fruit stalks are yellowish to reddish. Fruits are yellowish-green, turning blue, then ripening to shiny bluish-black. The fruits are very bitter, with thin flesh in proportion to the pits, and are generally regarded as inedible.

SEASON: Downy arrowwood produces flat-topped clusters of showy white flowers, which smell unpleasant, in early summer. Fruits ripen in late summer.

COMPARE: Blackhaw (pg. 292) produces similar clusters of black fruit, but the leaves are larger, with fine teeth; blackhaw fruits are larger. Several arrowwood in our area have blue fruits; please see pg. 232.

NOTES: Arrowwood was used to make arrows, because the branches are long and straight, with no tapering. Fruits of downy arrowwood were reportedly eaten by American Indian peoples in Canada (*Traditional Plant Foods of Canadian Indigenous Peoples,* Harriet V. Kuhnlein and Nancy J. Turner). Sometimes spelled *V. rafinesqueanum.*

green = key identification feature

LARGE
WOODY SHRUB

OPPOSITE
LEAVES

LATE SUMMER
TO EARLY FALL

Common Buckthorn

Rhamnus cathartica

HABITAT: Open hardwood forests, prairie areas, fields, forest edges, urban parks, shelterbelts, floodplains, ravines and fence rows. Prefers partial shade but can tolerate moist or dry conditions.

GROWTH: A large, multi-stemmed shrub with a spreading crown, sometimes appearing to be a small tree; up to 20 feet in height but usually much shorter. Bark is gray to brown; older stems are roughly textured, with long, corky protrusions. Twigs often have a spine at the tip, giving the species its common name.

LEAVES: Dark, glossy green, broadly oval, with a pointed tip and a broad base; leaves grow oppositely on long petioles (stemlets). Leaves are 1½ to 3 inches long, and roughly two-thirds as wide; both surfaces are hairless. Edges are finely toothy; each leaf has three to five pairs of deep veins that curve in toward the tip to follow the edge of the leaf. Leaves remain green late into fall, long after most other shrubs have lost their leaves.

FRUIT: Glossy, round black drupes, about ¼ inch in diameter, grow on thin stemlets in dense clusters at leaf axils, or singly along the stems. The fruits are strongly cathartic, and are considered toxic.

SEASON: Common buckthorn ripens in late summer to early fall.

COMPARE: Lanceleaf buckthorn (pg. 276) has very narrow leaves that are one-third as wide as they are long. Glossy buckthorn (pg. 290) has smooth-edged leaves that are typically alternate; leaf undersides are hairy, and the twigs are lacking the spine at the tip. Dogwood (pgs. 230, 234 and 310) have leaves with similar veins, but the fruits are borne in umbrella-shaped clusters.

NOTES: Common buckthorn is a non-native species, imported in the late 1800s from Europe for use as a landscape plant. It has naturalized, and is considered invasive throughout most of its range. It spreads rapidly, crowding out native plants.

green = key identification feature

LARGE
WOODY SHRUB

ALTERNATE
LEAVES

LATE SUMMER
TO EARLY FALL

Chokeberry –OR– **Aronia**

Aronia melanocarpa

HABITAT: Thickets, mixed-wood or hardwood forests, waste ground, urban parks. Tolerates a wide range of conditions, from dry to moist.

GROWTH: A leggy, native shrub, up to 10 feet in height but usually shorter. Stems near the base are leafless, giving the shrub an open appearance at the bottom. Young stems are reddish-brown; older stems have noticeable lenticels (breathing pores). Chokeberry produces suckers (shoots) and may form thickets.

LEAVES: Glossy, bright green leaves with finely toothed edges are 2 to 3 inches long and two-thirds as wide; they are oval, broadest at or above the midpoint, tapering on both ends. Tips are pointed; the undersides are lighter in color. Leaves grow alternately on short petioles (stemlets) that are often reddish. The midribs on the upper surface have small, hair-like glands (visible with a lens). Leaves turn red in fall.

FRUIT: A glossy, round pome that is black when ripe. The bottom has five distinct indentations in a star pattern; it looks a bit like a pucker. Fruits are ¼ to ⅜ inch in diameter, and grow in small clusters on long, thin stemlets from the end of a branch. The fruit is acrid, but is tasty when sweetened; its seeds are so soft that they are unnoticeable. There are several woody shrubs with inedible black fruits that could be confused with chokeberries; please see below.

SEASON: Fruits ripen in late summer to early fall, and may persist on the plant through winter.

COMPARE: Buckthorn (pgs. 276, 280, 290) have inedible black fruits; their leaves are similar, but fruits grow singly or in clusters from the leaf axils rather than at branch tips. Like chokeberry, fruits of the *Cotoneaster* species have a star-shaped indentation on the bottom, but its twigs and young leaves are hairy; its fruits are inedible. *Cotoneaster* is a cultivated plant that is found only rarely in the wild in our area.

NOTES: Aronia juice is popular in Europe and making its way into health-food markets here. Chokeberry is considered endangered in Iowa.

green = key identification feature

LARGE
WOODY SHRUB

OPPOSITE
LEAVES

LATE SUMMER
TO EARLY FALL

* see below

European Privet –AND–
Border Privet

Ligustrum vulgare, L. obtusifolium

HABITAT: Privet are non-native shrubs that have escaped into the wild, especially close to urban areas where they are planted as ornamentals. Two appear in our area: European privet (*Ligustrum vulgare*) and border privet (*L. obtusifolium*). They can be found in thickets, disturbed areas and bottomland forests, as well as along roadsides and forest edges. They prefer sun, but tolerate shade in areas of rich soil.

GROWTH: Privet are leafy, multi-branched shrubs that may grow to 15 feet in height and width; they spread by suckering and often form dense thickets. Branches are brownish-gray, with numerous lenticels (breathing pores); they tend to be long and arching. The trunk is often hard to see due to all the leaves; it is gray and rough but not fissured.

LEAVES: Glossy, oval to lance-shaped leaves that taper on both ends grow oppositely on short, hairy petioles (stemlets); edges are untoothed. Leaves often grow at almost a right angle to the branch. Leaf shape is variable among the privets. Those of European privet are typically narrower, up to 2½ inches in length and one-quarter as wide; border privet's leaves are typically a bit shorter and one-half as wide, with a rounded tip. Border privet leaves are hairy underneath, particularly on the midvein; undersides are hairless on European privet.

FRUIT: Oval to round drupes, ¼ to ⅓ inch in length, grow in large clusters at branch tips; they also are scattered in smaller clusters along the branches. Ripe fruits are glossy black to purplish-black. The fruits are considered toxic, reportedly causing intestinal problems.

SEASON: Fruits ripen from late summer to early fall, and may persist through winter; leaves may remain green through winter.

COMPARE: Lanceleaf buckthorn (pg. 276) and other buckthorns have black berries, but leaf edges are toothy and the plants aren't as full as privet.

NOTES: Considered an invasive species due to its aggressive growth.

green = key identification feature   * combined range

Border privet (unripe)

European privet

TOXIC

LARGE
WOODY SHRUB

OPPOSITE
LEAVES

LATE SUMMER
TO EARLY FALL

* see below

Jetbead

Rhodotypos scandens

HABITAT: This Asian native occasionally escapes cultivation in our area, and may be found in parklands, abandoned fields and thickets, especially those near urban areas, where it is planted as an ornamental. An adaptable plant, it tolerates full sun to moderate shade, and can grow in moist or dry areas.

GROWTH: A mounded, leafy shrub, up to 6 feet in height but usually shorter; it is typically wider than it is tall. Branches are brownish to grayish and smooth; they are often long, and gracefully arched. White, four-petaled flowers, 1½ inches across, appear at branch tips in late spring to early summer.

LEAVES: Coarse, oval leaves, broadest below the midpoint, grow oppositely on very short petioles (stemlets); the tip is pointed, and the base slightly rounded. Leaves are 2 to 4 inches in length and one-half as wide; they are doubly toothed, with deeply impressed parallel veins.

FRUIT: Glossy, rounded berries, about ⅓ inch across, grow in tight clusters at the branch tips. There are typically four berries per cluster, occasionally three; four brownish petal-like sepals are present at the base of the berries. The berries are black when ripe; they are toxic at all stages, and can cause respiratory difficulties, intestinal problems and other symptoms.

SEASON: Berries are red in midsummer, ripening to glossy jet-black in late summer to early fall; they usually persist through winter.

COMPARE: Flowering dogwood (pg. 184) has similar tightly bunched fruits, but they are red when ripe; flowering dogwood is a small tree.

NOTES: Unlike many other non-native plants which escape cultivation, jetbead does not seem to be an invasive plant; it is not widely found in the wild. It is likely that wildlife use the plants for cover.

green = key identification feature   * specific MO locations not available

LARGE WOODY SHRUB

ALTERNATE LEAVES

MID SUMMER TO FALL

Farkleberry

Deerberry

Farkleberry
–AND– **Deerberry**

Vaccinium arboreum, V. stamineum

HABITAT: These native shrubs are found in open, rocky areas with acidic soil, including glades, hardwood or mixed-wood forests, streambanks, slopes and upland ridges. They prefer sun or dappled shade.

GROWTH: Farkleberry (also called sparkleberry) is a large shrub that can reach 30 feet in height; deerberry can grow to 10 feet. Both are rather twisted and gnarly, especially older specimens. Twigs are green to reddish-brown, and hairy when young. The trunk has rough-textured brown or gray bark that is flaky or shreddy; the inner bark is reddish.

LEAVES: Oval to egg-shaped leaves, with a tapering base, grow alternately on short petioles (stemlets); they are 1 to 2½ inches in length and one-half as wide, and broadest above the middle. Farkleberry leaves are leathery and glossy, with widely spaced veins; most have a rounded tip. Deerberry leaves have a pointed tip; the underside is hairy, and the smaller veins are very close together.

FRUIT: Round berries with a five-pointed crown on the bottom grow in loose clusters on thin stemlets from leaf axils. Farkleberries are about ⅜ inch across, and glossy black when ripe; deerberry are slightly smaller, and ripen to purplish-black with a dusty bloom, although some fail to ripen, remaining green. Both are edible, although farkleberries may be bitter and mealy. Deerberries are not as tasty as low-growing blueberries (pg. 226) but can be used in similar ways. Several tall shrubs in our area have dark-colored fruits that are inedible; see below.

SEASON: Deerberry are ripe in mid to late summer; farkleberry ripen in fall, and its leaves often remain green into the winter.

COMPARE: These fruits resemble several inedible or toxic fruits found in our area (glossy buckthorn, pg. 290; common buckthorn, pg. 280; privet, pg. 284), but none have a crown on the bottom.

NOTES: Farkleberries may be tough and bitter; try a few before picking.

green = key identification feature

Widely spaced veins, hairy twig of farkleberry

Farkleberry

LARGE SHRUB
OR SMALL TREE

ALTERNATE
LEAVES (TYP.)

SUMMER

• see below

Glossy Buckthorn (ripe)

Frangula alnus

HABITAT: Open woods, wetlands, abandoned fields. Also found along roads, on the edges of power line cuts, next to ponds and streams, and along paths. Tends to form thickets. Also called *Rhamnus frangula*.

GROWTH: A large, multi-stemmed shrub up to 20 feet in height; sometimes appears to be a small tree. Branches often droop down over paths, making the colorful fruits very obvious. The bark is smooth and grayish-brown, with noticeable lenticels (breathing pores) that are slightly raised.

LEAVES: Typically alternate, but may be opposite; smooth edges. Deep green above, lighter and slightly hairy below, with deep veins that form a V at the midrib, then curve near the edges to follow the contour of the leaf. Leaves are oblong with a pointed tip, 2 to 4 inches long and one-half as wide, widest at the midpoint or slightly toward the tip. Leaves turn yellow in fall.

FRUIT: The ¼-inch berries grow in the leaf axils; often seen as a pair, but may also be single or in small groups. The berries are green with a small dot at the base when they first appear, developing a red blush and then changing to mottled red before ripening to black. They are also included in the red section of this book (pg. 168) because they are so frequently seen in the red stage. The berries are mildly toxic.

SEASON: Fruits are on the plant from early through late summer. Green, red and black fruits may all be present on the plant at the same time.

COMPARE: Common buckthorn (pg. 280) has opposite, toothy leaves that are more rounded, and the ends of the stems have a sharp spine. Dogwood (pgs. 230, 234 and 310) have leaves with similar veins, but the fruits are borne in umbrella-shaped clusters.

NOTES: This species was imported into the United States as an ornamental in the 1800s. It is considered invasive in many areas as it spreads rapidly, crowding out native plants.

green = key identification feature   * specific IA locations not available

LARGE SHRUB
OR SMALL TREE

OPPOSITE
LEAVES

LATE SUMMER
TO EARLY FALL

• see below

Blackhaw   Nannyberry

Blackhaw
–AND– Nannyberry

Viburnum prunifolium, V. lentago

HABITAT: Openings and edges in moist, well-drained hardwood and mixed-wood forests; also found along roadsides and streambanks.

GROWTH: These native plants are open and multi-stemmed, up to 20 feet in height; they are often leggy and unkempt-looking. Stems are tan to reddish-brown; tips develop a long, pointed "dragon's claw" in fall.

LEAVES: Smooth, light green leaves grow oppositely; they are oval, 1 to 4 inches in length and roughly one-half as wide. Bases are rounded; tips are pointed, with the tip of a nannyberry leaf being slightly more acute than that of blackhaw. Leaves of both have finely toothed edges. The petioles (stemlets) are a key point of differentiation between these two species; they are broad with smooth edges on blackhaw, while those of nannyberry have wavy edges. Leaves of both turn red in fall.

FRUIT: Oval to round drupes, about ½ inch long, grow in loose, flat clusters that hang from stem forks or tips; individual fruits may fall off before ripe, making the cluster look more open. Green fruits develop a reddish blush, then ripen to a dull blue-black, eventually becoming black and wrinkled. Ripe nannyberries and blackhaws are delicious raw or cooked; the pit is a nuisance. There are no toxic look-alikes; some similar-looking *Viburnum* such as downy arrowwood (pg. 278) taste awful, but they aren't dangerous to sample—only unpleasant.

SEASON: Nannyberries and blackhaws ripen in late summer to early fall, and often persist through winter.

COMPARE: Two other *Viburnum* with similar fruits are found occasionally in Illinois; leaves help distinguish them. Wayfaringtree (*V. lantana*) appears very wrinkly between the veins; undersides are hairy. Withe-rod (*V. cassinoides*) have rounded teeth and round petioles. Withe-rod fruits are delicious; those of the wayfaringtree taste unpleasant.

NOTES: A delicious fruit, worth the trouble to remove the pit.

green = key identification feature   * specific IA locations not available

Nannyberry

Smooth petiole on blackhaw

Wavy petiole, dragon's claw on nannyberry

LARGE SHRUB
OR SMALL TREE

ALTERNATE
COMPOUND
LEAVES

FALL

Devil's Walking Stick

Aralia spinosa

HABITAT: This native plant is found in areas with moist, sandy or rocky soil, including disturbed areas, open woodlands, thickets, clearings, ravines, slopes and forest edges. It grows in full sun to partial shade.

GROWTH: A wickedly thorny large shrub or small tree, growing to 30 feet high. It has an open, flat crown; trees are top-heavy, often with few branches at the base. Twigs, stems and even the leaf stalks are armed with sharp thorns. Young stems are green; older bark is brownish to tan. Large clusters of white flowers are borne at the branch tips.

LEAVES: Twice- or thrice-compound leaves, up to 4 feet in length and nearly as wide, grow alternately on leaf stalks that clasp the branch; from a distance, the leaves are open, with a lace-like appearance. Each branch of the leaf is 1 to 2 feet in length, with five or six pairs of heart-shaped leaflets and a terminal leaflet that are 1 to 3 inches in length and about half as wide. Leaves turn yellow or reddish in fall.

FRUIT: Oval drupes, ⅛ to ¼ inch in length, grow in large clusters on lacy, reddish-pink or purplish stemlets at branch tips. The fruits are black when ripe, but are quickly eaten by birds, leaving behind the lacy network of stemlets. The fruits are inedible, and may be mildly toxic.

SEASON: Flowers appear in mid to late summer; fruits ripen in fall.

COMPARE: It is difficult to distinguish the native devil's walking stick from the related, but non-native, angelica (*A. elata*), found in our area only rarely in Illinois. Leaflets of devil's walking stick have a short but visible petiole (stemlet), while those of angelica attach directly to the stem. Also, the leaf veins of devil's walking stick stop short of the leaf edge, while on angelica, the veins extend to the edge. Another viciously thorny plant, Hercules' club (*Zanthoxylum clava-herculis*), is similar in overall appearance and thorniness; it is found south of our region. The clusters of small black berries on lacy pinkish stems resemble common elderberry (pg. 204), but the similarities end there.

NOTES: Tender young leaves can be cooked and eaten (Steven Brill).

green = key identification feature

Main stem

Thorns on leaf stalk

TREE

ALTERNATE
LEAVES

MID TO LATE
SUMMER

Black Cherry –OR– Rum Cherry
Prunus serotina

HABITAT: Sun-dappled hardwood and mixed-wood forests; edge habitat.

GROWTH: A tall, stately native tree, up to 90 feet high and 50 feet wide but typically smaller; when young, may appear as a small shrub. Young stems are reddish-brown or gray, with prominent lenticels (breathing pores); older bark is dark gray, with curling, scaly plates.

LEAVES: Smooth, glossy leaves are oval, with tapered bases and long, pointed tips; edges are finely toothed. Leaves are 2 to 5 inches long, one-half to one-third as wide, and dark green above, paler below. The base of the midrib on the underside has **fine reddish hairs** (visible with a lens); this is one of the easiest ways to positively identify a black cherry. Leaves grow alternately on a petiole (stemlet).

FRUIT: Round, reddish-black drupes grow in **racemes** (long clusters of multiple fruits) from leaf axils. Fruits are about ⅓ inch in diameter; they are glossy but opaque. Fruit stemlets and the fruiting stalk are often reddish-purple. Black cherries are sweet and delicious, but the pit is fairly large in proportion to the flesh so the fruit is usually juiced, or pulped to make jam. There are no toxic look-alikes that are large trees, but there are several woody shrubs with inedible black fruits that could be confused with black cherries; please see below.

SEASON: Black cherries ripen in mid to late summer.

COMPARE: Chokecherries (pgs. 154) have edible fruits that grow in racemes, but leaves are proportionally wider and lack the hairs on the midrib. Buckthorn (pgs. 276, 280 and 290) have mildly toxic black fruits; leaves are somewhat similar, but the fruits grow singly or in clusters from the leaf axils rather than in racemes.

NOTES: Black cherry leaves and pits contain hydrocyanic acid, a cyanide-producing compound. The leaves and pits should never be eaten, and care should be taken to avoid crushing cherry pits when juicing the fruits. Cooking, drying or freezing eliminates the acid.

green = key identification feature

Hairs at base of midrib

TREE

ALTERNATE LEAVES

LATE SUMMER TO EARLY FALL

Hackberry

Sugarberry

Hackberry –AND– Sugarberry

Celtis occidentalis, C. laevigata

HABITAT: These native trees are found in rich valleys and bottomlands, hardwood forests, waste ground, fencerows, ditches and urban areas. They prefer full sun and moist soils, but can adapt to drier areas.

GROWTH: Hackberry (*Celtis occidentalis*) is 40 to 60 feet in height with almost equal spread; sugarberry (*C. laevigata*) can be up to 80 feet. Lower branches of both often droop toward the ground. Young stems are reddish, with a zigzag habit; branches are brown, with light-colored lenticels (breathing pores). Bark on the trunk is dark gray; hackberry bark is ridged and warty, while sugarberry is warty but lacks the ridges.

LEAVES: Rough-textured, dull green, alternate leaves are shaped like an elongated heart, with a sharply pointed tip; undersides are pale. Leaves are 2 to 5 inches in length and about one-half as wide; they are widest near the base, which is rounded and often slightly angled. Three of the leaf veins meet at the base of the leaf. Edges of hackberry leaves have large, pointed teeth except around the base, which has smooth edges; sugarberry leaves are toothy only on the top half.

FRUIT: Round drupes, ¼ to ⅓ inch in diameter, grow singly or in pairs on long stemlets from the leaf axils. They are orangish-red in summer, ripening in fall. Ripe hackberries are purplish-black, while ripe sugarberries are more reddish. The flesh is thin in comparison to the size of the pit; however, it is sweet and delicious. There are no toxic look-alikes that grow on trees.

SEASON: Fruits ripen in late summer to early fall, and they may persist through winter.

COMPARE: Black cherry (pg. 296) is a tree with small, round black fruits; however, its leaves are narrower, and the fruits grow in long clusters.

NOTES: Hackberries are often planted in urban parks and along streets because they are fast-growing shade trees and resist storm damage.

green = key identification feature

Ripe hackberries

Hackberry bark

Sugarberry bark

Unripe sugarberries

TREE

ALTERNATE LEAVES

FALL

Gum Bumelia

Sideroxylon lanuginosum

HABITAT: This native tree grows in open woods, on hillsides and in rocky areas. It grows best in sunlight, but will tolerate moderate shade. It is very resistant to drought.

GROWTH: A medium tree, up to 60 feet tall but usually shorter. Young twigs are gray and hairy; side branches are hairless, and often have white blotches. Larger branches are dark gray, with orangish streaks; they are often gently curved. Gum bumelia often has multiple trunks, which may curve slightly; the bark is gray and heavily fissured. Twigs are usually tipped with spines; side branches have numerous thorns.

LEAVES: Paddle-shaped leaves, 1 to 3 inches in length and one-third to one-half as wide, have a tapered base and a broad, rounded tip; they grow alternately, or in clusters at the tips of small branches. Leaves are glossy and deep green on top; undersides are paler and covered with dense, felt-like hairs, and young leaves are hairy on both sides. The midvein is prominent, especially underneath; petioles are short and velvety. Leaf edges are smooth.

FRUIT: Oval drupes, ½ to ¾ inch long, grow in clusters on short stalks originating in leaf axils. Fruits have a single stone, which is fairly large in proportion to the flesh. Immature fruits are greenish, turning reddish-purple before ripening to black. The fruits are edible, but may cause stomach upset or dizziness if many are eaten. It's best to consider them inedible.

SEASON: Fragrant yellow flowers appear in midsummer; fruits ripen in fall.

COMPARE: Buckthorn bumelia (*S. lycioides*) is a related, similar plant, found in our area in only a few counties of southern Illinois, and in Missouri's bootheel; its leaves are tapered at the tip rather than rounded. Numerous other shrubs and trees in our area have oval, black fruits, but none have the paddle-shaped leaves of gum bumelia.

NOTES: Also called gum bully or chittamwood; some texts list this as *Bumelia lanuginosa*. Gum bumelia is considered endangered in Illinois.

green = key identification feature

Tree with immature fruits

Fruit

TENDER
LEAFY PLANT

ALTERNATE
LEAVES

LATE SUMMER
TO EARLY FALL

Canada Mayflower
–OR– False Lily of the Valley *Maianthemum canadense*

HABITAT: This native species is found in mixed, hardwood or coniferous forests; also occasionally found near bogs and swampy areas. It can grow in sun or shade.

GROWTH: An understory plant that is 3 to 7 inches in height. Thin stems grow from shallow underground rhizomes (root-bearing stems) that often form large colonies. Flowers and fruit are borne in clusters at the top of stems bearing two or three leaves. Stems with a single leaf do not flower.

LEAVES: One to three bright green, shiny leaves grow alternately from a single stem. Leaves are heart-shaped, with a deeply grooved midline and parallel veins that curve to meet at the sharply pointed tip. Bases are rounded and appear to clasp the stem. Most leaves appear to have a slight notch where the base joins the stem. Leaves are 1 to 3 inches long, and nearly as wide at the base. Edges are smooth.

FRUIT: Shiny, round berries are ⅛ to ¼ inch wide and cream-colored with red speckles most of the season. By late summer or early fall, berries soften and turn solid red. The ripe berries are bittersweet in flavor; they reportedly cause diarrhea, and consumption is not advised.

SEASON: In late spring or early summer, a cluster of white flowers grows at the top of stems bearing two or three leaves; the flowers turn into speckled cream-colored berries by midsummer. Berries turn pinkish with red speckles, then ripen to solid red by late summer or early fall.

COMPARE: Bunchberry (pg. 102) has leaves that somewhat resemble those of Canada mayflower, but bunchberry plants have groupings of four to six leaves, with pronounced veins. Please also see the discussion of common false Solomon's seal and similar plants on pg. 36.

NOTES: Ruffed grouse and woodland rodents eat the berries.

green = key identification feature

Ripe fruit

TENDER
LEAFY PLANT

ALTERNATE
COMPOUND
LEAVES

MID TO LATE
SUMMER

White Baneberry
–OR– Doll's Eyes   *Actaea pachypoda*

HABITAT: This native plant grows in shady areas in moist hardwood and mixed forests. Often found in dappled woods alongside bracken fern and large-leaved aster.

GROWTH: Two to four doubly compound leaves, each up to 15 inches long, grow alternately on the main stem; total height is 1 to 2½ feet. Flowers grow on a separate, leafless stalk that branches off one of the leaf stalks, and generally rise above the surrounding leaves.

LEAVES: Three large compound leaflets grow on each of the long leaf stalks attached to the main stem; each has three or five smooth, sharply toothed leaflets oppositely attached by short stalks.

FRUIT: Firm, glossy white berry about ⅜ inch long, slightly oval to round with a shallow vertical groove. Each berry has a large, oval black dot at the bottom. The berries grow in a cluster at the top of the thin flower stalk, and are attached to the stalk by thick stemlets with slight knobs on both ends; stemlets are usually reddish-pink. Baneberries are toxic and should never be eaten.

SEASON: Berries ripen in mid to late summer.

COMPARE: The related red baneberry (pg. 94) looks similar, but the flower stalk and berry stemlets are thin and greenish; those of white bane-berry are much thicker and usually reddish-pink. Red baneberries generally have red berries, although they are sometimes white; regardless of color, the dot on the bottom of the red baneberry is much smaller than that on a white baneberry. Blue cohosh (pg. 218) has a similar form, but the leaves are rounded; fruits are larger and are blue when ripe.

NOTES: All parts of the plant are toxic. Ingestion of the berries leads to dizziness, vomiting or cardiac arrest; contact with leaves may cause skin irritation in sensitive individuals. Birds eat the berries with no ill effect, helping to disperse the seeds.

green = key identification feature

–OR–

WOODY VINE | SMALL WOODY SHRUB | ALTERNATE COMPOUND LEAVES | LATE SUMMER TO FALL

*see below
Western   Eastern

Poison Ivy

Toxicodendron rydbergii, T. radicans

HABITAT: Moist areas with moderate sun, such as road ditches, open woodlands, fencelines, swampy areas and stream banks; also found in agricultural fields, sandy areas and disturbed sites.

GROWTH: Two varieties are native to our region: western (*Toxicodendron rydbergii*) and eastern (*T. radicans*). Western poison ivy grows as a shrub from 1 to 4 feet high, but can also appear as a tender leafy plant; eastern poison ivy is a climbing, perennial vine with stems that are often thick and hairy. Both have the classic three-part leaf configuration leading to the old saying, "Leaves of three, let it be."

LEAVES: Three-part leaves grow on the ends of long stalks attached alternately to the stem. Leaflets have irregular toothy or wavy edges; the petiole (stemlet) of the middle leaflet is longer than those of the side leaflets. Leaflets of western poison ivy are 2 to 4 inches long; those of eastern poison ivy are often up to 8 inches in length. Leaves of western poison ivy turn red in fall; those of eastern turn yellowish.

FRUIT: The round, ridged berries, 1/8 to 3/16 inch across, are greenish when immature, ripening to white or yellowish (see pg. 48 for a photo of eastern poison ivy in its green stage). Berries of western poison ivy grow in upright clusters near the main stem; those of eastern poison ivy grow from leaf axils in large, loose clusters. All parts of both plants are toxic and may cause a painful rash if touched; smoke from burning poison ivy can cause a severe allergic reaction.

SEASON: Berries develop in late summer, and persist through fall.

COMPARE: Atlantic poison oak (*T. pubescens*) is very similar to western poison ivy, but with hairy petioles and fruits; in our area, it is found in a few counties in southern Missouri and Illinois. Black raspberry (pg. 258) and other *Rubus* have toothy 3-part leaflets, but they are brambles (vine-like shrubs) with thorny stems; fruits are compound drupes.

NOTES: The toxic compound in poison ivy, urushiol, remains active on everything it touches, until washed off.

green = key identification feature   * specific IL locations not available

Western poison ivy

Ripe berries of western
poison ivy

PARASITIC
SUBSHRUB

OPPOSITE
LEAVES

EARLY
WINTER

Oak Mistletoe
Phoradendron leucarpum

HABITAT: This native plant, also called American mistletoe, is a parasitic subshrub that attaches itself to oak, red maple, hickory, pecan, elm and other hardwood trees; it has no intrinsic habitat of its own.

GROWTH: A small, evergreen shrub found growing on branches of hardwood trees, mistletoe is spread by birds, who deposit the seeds on tree branches either by wiping their beaks to remove the sticky pulp containing the seeds, or through droppings containing the undigested seeds. The seeds adhere to the branches and develop roots, which parasitize the host tree. Mistletoe has fleshy green stems, and grows in large, rounded clumps up to 3 feet across; it does not develop into a woody shrub-like plant, although older stems may develop a brown web-like covering that resembles bark. It is typically noticed as a cluster of green leaves high up in hardwood trees, after the host trees lose their leaves in fall.

LEAVES: Paddle-shaped, leathery leaves with parallel veins running from base to tip, are up to 2 inches in length and about two-thirds as wide; they are widest above the midpoint. The tip is rounded, and the base is sharply tapered. Leaves grow oppositely on very short petioles (stemlets), and remain green all year.

FRUIT: Translucent, glossy white berries, ¼ to ⅜ inch across, grow in clusters on stemlets along the branches. The berries are juicy, with a single, ¼-inch-long seed and extremely sticky pulp. Berries and all other parts of the plant are toxic to humans.

SEASON: Mistletoe berries ripen in early winter, and remain on the plants through late winter, unless eaten by birds.

COMPARE: With its parasitic growth habit, its location high in trees, and its glossy white berries, mistletoe is unlike anything found in our area.

NOTES: Mistletoe sprigs are used as holiday decorations; retailers sometimes replace the berries with plastic berries to prevent poisoning and to extend the shelf life of the decoration.

green = key identification feature

Oak mistletoe growing on an Osage orange tree

LARGE WOODY SHRUB

OPPOSITE LEAVES

MIDSUMMER TO EARLY FALL

Gray   Rough-leaved   Red-osier

Dogwood (several)
Cornus spp.

HABITAT: Three species of native dogwood with white fruits inhabit our region: gray dogwood (*Cornus racemosa*), rough-leaved dogwood (*C. drummondii*) and red-osier dogwood (*C. sericea*). Gray dogwood is found in well-drained upland forests; the other dogwoods listed here prefer slightly damp soil, and are often found in swampy areas.

GROWTH: A bushy shrub, typically 4 to 6 feet in height but sometimes much larger; gray dogwood may grow to 15 feet. Often seen as a spreading thicket. The color of young stems helps identify the species: gray dogwood are bronze, rough-leaved dogwood are brownish-red, and red-osier dogwood are bright red or green splotched with red. Young stems are hairy.

LEAVES: Oppositely attached, 1 to 3 inches long and about one-half as wide, with smooth edges, silvery-green undersides with fine hairs. Distinct veins curve in towards the pointy tip. Leaf tops are smooth on gray dogwood, while those of rough dogwood leaves are coarsely textured; red-osier leaves appear puckered between the veins.

FRUIT: White, round drupes, ¼ inch across, with a small protrusion on the bottom; fruits of red-osier dogwood may be tinged with blue. The fruits grow in clusters on the ends of branching stemlets. The fruit stemlets of gray and rough-leaved dogwood are red, while those of red-osier dogwood are purplish. Dogwood fruits are inedible.

SEASON: Fruits mature from midsummer to early fall; gray dogwood ripens later than other dogwoods in the same area.

COMPARE: Roundleaf dogwood (pg. 230) has light blue fruits which may resemble those of red-osier dogwood; however, the leaves of round-leaf dogwood are wider and rough on the top, the stems are green with purple blotches, and the fruit stemlets are red.

NOTES: Dogwood fruits are eaten by many birds including cardinals, woodpeckers, wood ducks and upland birds; deer browse on the fruits, leaves and twigs. Dogwood is a host to the spring azure butterfly.

green = key identification feature

Gray dogwood

Red-osier dogwood

NOT EDIBLE

LARGE
WOODY SHRUB

OPPOSITE
LEAVES

LATE SUMMER
TO EARLY FALL

Western

• see below
Common

Western Snowberry –AND–
Common Snowberry *Symphoricarpos occidentalis, S. albus*

HABITAT: Two native snowberry plants are found in our area: western snowberry (*Symphoricarpos occidentalis*, also called wolfberry) and common snowberry (*S. albus*). Both are found in open woods, ravines and prairies, as well as on hillsides and along edges of grasslands. They prefer well-drained soil, but will tolerate somewhat damp conditions.

GROWTH: Bushy, rounded shrubs; western snowberry is typically 2 to 6 feet in height, while common snowberry is 3½ feet or less. Both often form thickets. Twigs are slender and reddish-brown, with fine hairs; older branches are gray and have shreddy bark.

LEAVES: Oval to egg-shaped leaves grow oppositely on short, hairy petioles (stemlets); edges are often wavy. Leaves of western snowberry are up to 4 inches in length and roughly two-thirds as wide; common snowberry leaves are shorter, generally no more than 1½ inches long. Upper surfaces of both are blue-green to dark green, and may have scattered fine hairs; lower surfaces are generally hairy.

FRUIT: Roughly spherical, waxy white drupes, with a small floral remnant on the base, grow in tight clusters at the ends of branches or in leaf axils. Western snowberry fruits are round or slightly flattened, up to ¼ inch across; they are typically creamy white when young, turning purplish with age. Common snowberry fruits are frequently lumpy and misshapen, up to ⅜ inch across; they are usually brilliant white. Fruits of both are mildly bitter and are generally considered inedible; some sources list them as toxic.

SEASON: The fruits, which follow white to pinkish flowers, form in late summer, and may persist through winter on leafless branches.

COMPARE: Coralberry (pg. 146) is a related plant; its fruits are small and red.

NOTES: A winter food source for birds, including thrashers and many upland birds. Common snowberry is listed as endangered in Illinois.

green = key identification feature   * specific IA locations not available

Western snowberry

Common snowberry

LARGE SHRUB
OR SMALL TREE

ALTERNATE
LEAVES

LATE SUMMER
TO EARLY FALL

American Snowbell

Styrax americanus

HABITAT: This native plant grows in swamps dominated by bald cypress or tupelo; also found in floodplain forests, oxbow lakes, moist open woods, wooded streambanks and areas that are seasonally wet. It requires moist soil and prefers partial shade.

GROWTH: A large woody shrub or small tree, up to 15 feet in height but often shorter. It has numerous thin branches, and an open, rounded crown. Bark is dark gray or brownish, and is smooth when young, developing shallow fissures with age; twigs are reddish-brown to grayish, and may be hairy. Multiple bell-shaped white flowers with five narrow, curled-back petals grow singly on short stemlets or in racemes (long clusters of multiple flowers) originating from the leaf axils; the fragrant flowers dangle beneath the branches, making a delightful display in late spring to early summer.

LEAVES: Smooth, dark green leaves grow alternately on short, broad petioles (stemlets); undersides are paler and typically downy. Leaves are up to 3 inches in length and typically one-third as wide, broadest at the midpoint, with a tapering base and pointed tip. Edges often have shallow, irregular teeth above the base, but may be smooth. The leaves typically stand upright on the stems.

FRUIT: A round, leathery drupe, ¼ to ½ inch across and sometimes slightly flattened or lumpy. It has a green, five-lobed cap where it connects to the stemlet, and there is often a thread-like tail on the end. The fruit is greenish when immature, ripening to white. It is inedible.

SEASON: Flowers are present from late spring to early summer; the fruits ripen in late summer, and split open into three parts in the fall.

COMPARE: When American snowbell is bearing flowers or fruit, there is nothing in our area that would be confused with it.

NOTES: American snowbell is rare in Illinois; some sources feel it may have disappeared from the wild, although it is still listed as present in the USDA PLANTS database and the Illinois Plant Information Network.

green = key identification feature

TREE

ALTERNATE
COMPOUND
LEAVES

SUMMER
THROUGH FALL

Poison Sumac

Toxicodendron vernix

HABITAT: Prefers shade and damp soil, and is often found at the edges of swamps or in poorly drained woods and bottomlands.

GROWTH: A small native tree up to 20 feet high, sometimes more like a large shrub, with red leaf stalks at the center of its compound leaves. Bark is grayish-brown and blotchy, with small raised bumps. Poison sumac often sends out branches from the base of the main trunk. Broken stems ooze a dark sap that is toxic.

LEAVES: Compound leaves grow alternately. Each leaf is 8 to 13 inches long, and has seven to 13 leaflets on short petioles, growing on a red central leaf stalk. Leaflets are bright green, 2 to 4 inches long, smooth in texture with smooth edges, and may be shiny on top. Poison sumac is very colorful in fall, with leaflets ranging in hue from yellow to orange to red to purple.

FRUIT: Round drupes are shiny and green when unripe, turning whitish-yellow by late summer; ¼ to ⅓ inch across. The fruits hang down in long, open clusters attached to leafless stems.

SEASON: Fruits ripen in late summer and may persist on the plant through winter, long after the leaves have fallen.

COMPARE: Smooth and staghorn sumac (pg. 188) have orange-to-red fruits; leaves have more leaflets, and leaf edges are toothed.

NOTES: All parts of poison sumac are toxic, and can cause severe allergic reactions. The plant can be identified from a distance by the red compound leaf stalk, green to white fruits growing in a long cluster, and bright green or autumn-colored compound leaves. Stay away when you see these characteristics, as sensitive individuals may have a reaction merely by being close to the plant without even touching it. Burning the plants can cause respiratory distress in individuals a good distance away. Poison sumac is sometimes listed as *Rhus vernix*. No matter what it is called, this is a plant to avoid.

green = key identification feature

Fruit cluster

HELPFUL RESOURCES AND BIBLIOGRAPHY

Information on wild plants is readily available in books, magazines and on the Internet. In general, information found on websites from University Extension Services, arboretums, colleges and other institutions of higher learning are generally more reliable than personal websites. Here is a list of some books and websites which provide good information, and which were helpful in writing this book.

Websites

Illinois Plant Information Network. (www.fs.fed.us/ne/delaware/ilpin/ilpin.html)

Illinois State Museum Herbarium Collection, Springfield, IL 62701. (museum.state.il.us/ismdepts/botany/herbarium/)

Illinois Wildflowers Info, Dr. John Hilty. (illinoiswildflowers.info)

Missouri Plants. (missouriplants.com)

U.S. Department of Agriculture, NRCS. 2008. The PLANTS Database. National Plant Data Center, Baton Rouge, LA 70874. (plants.usda.gov)

U.S. Forest Service, Washington, D.C. 20250. (www.fs.fed.us/)

University of Connecticut Plant Database, Dr. Mark H. Brand. (hort.uconn.edu/Plants/)

Vanderbilt University, Department of Biological Sciences, Nashville, TN 37240. (cas.vanderbilt.edu/bioimages)

Virginia Tech, College of Natural Resources, Forestry Department, Blacksburg, VA 24061. (www.cnr.vt.edu/)

Books

Brill, Steven. *Identifying and Harvesting Edible and Medicinal Plants in Wild (and Not So Wild) Places*. New York: William Morrow, 1994.

Bryson, Charles T. and Michael S. DeFelice, editors. *Weeds of the South*. Athens, GA: University of Georgia Press, 2009.

Eilers, Lawrence J. and Roosa, Dean M. *The Vascular Plants of Iowa*. Iowa City: University of Iowa Press, 1994.

Elias, Thomas S. and Dykeman, Peter A. *Field Guide to North American Edible Wild Plants*. New York: Outdoor Life Books, 1982.

Kershaw, Linda. *Trees of Illinois*. Auburn, WA: Lone Pine, 2007.

Kurz, Don. *Shrubs and Woody Vines of Missouri*. Jefferson City, MO: Missouri Department of Conservation, 2004 (second edition).

Marrone, Teresa. *Abundantly Wild: Collecting and Cooking Wild Edibles in the Upper Midwest*. Cambridge, MN: Adventure Publications, Inc., 2004.

Peterson, Lee Allen. *A Field Guide to Edible Wild Plants of Eastern and Central North America*. Boston: Houghton Mifflin Company, 1977.

Petrides, George A. *A Field Guide to Trees and Shrubs*. Boston: Houghton Mifflin, 1958.

Rose, Francis. *The Wild Flower Key*. London, England: Frederick Warne, The Penguin Group, 1981.

Sibley, David A. *The Sibley Guide to Trees*. New York: Alfred A. Knopf, 2009.

Sternberg, Guy and Wilson, James Wesley. *Native Trees for North American Landscapes: from the Atlantic to the Rockies*. Portland, OR: Timber Press, 2004.

Stevens, Russell L. and Coffey, Chuck R. *Trees, Shrubs and Woody Vines: A Pictorial Guide*. Ardmore, OK: The Samuel Roberts Noble Foundation, 2008.

Symonds, George W.D. *The Shrub Identification Book* and *The Tree Identification Book*. New York: Harper Collins, 1963 and 1958.

Tekiela, Stan. *Wildflowers of Minnesota* (and *Michigan, Ohio* and *Wisconsin*). Cambridge, MN: Adventure Publications, Inc., 1999–2001.

Thayer, Samuel. *The Forager's Harvest* and *Nature's Garden*. Birchwood, WI: Forager's Harvest, 2006 and 2010.

van der Linden, Peter J. and Farrar, Donald R., *Forest and Shade Trees of Iowa*. Ames, IA: Iowa State University Press, 1993.

GLOSSARY

Aggregate drupe: A fleshy fruit formed from a single flower, but composed of many drupes, each containing one seed; synonymous with compound drupe.

Alternate attachment: An arrangement of leaves in which individual leaves are attached to the stem in an alternating pattern, with some distance between each leaf. (*Compare:* Opposite attachment, Whorled attachment)

Annual: A plant which lives for one season only; reproduction is by seed rather than from roots. (*Compare:* Perennial)

Anther: The pollen-producing element of a flower.

Basal: Leaves growing at the base of a plant, often in a whorl or rosette pattern.

Berry: A simple, fleshy fruit containing one or more carpels, each with one or more seeds; the seeds are relatively soft. (*Compare:* Capsule, Cone, Drupe, Pepo, Pome, Pseudocarp)

Blade: The entire grouping of leaflets, stemlets and central leaf stalk that make up a compound leaf. The word "blade" is also used to describe the wide, flat part of a simple leaf.

Bloom: A light-colored or waxy coating on a fruit or stem, that gives it a dusty appearance.

Boreal forest: A forest of the far north, characterized by coniferous trees, infertile soil and long, cold winters; the boreal forest is south of the Arctic Circle, in an area formerly covered by glaciers.

Bract: A petal-like structure at the base of a flower.

Bramble: A sprawling, vine-like shrub with arching branches that are generally thorny or prickly.

Cane: A flexible, woody stem; usually used to describe brambles such as raspberries.

Capsule: A dry, non-fleshy fruit that splits at maturity to scatter seeds. (*Compare:* Berry, Cone, Drupe, Pepo, Pome, Pseudocarp)

Carpel: Part of the ovary of a plant, containing ovules (eggs).

Cathartic: Purgative; causing diarrhea or vomiting.

Catkin: A spike-like structure with tiny unisexual flowers, often having a fuzzy appearance.

Clasping: A leaf that attaches directly to the stem, with no leaf stalk; the base of the leaf clasps, or slightly surrounds, the stem but does not extend beyond it. (*Compare:* Peltate, Perfoliate, Sessile)

Cleft: A linear depression with smooth edges.

Compound drupe: A fleshy fruit formed from a single flower, but composed of many drupes, each containing one seed.

Compound leaf: A leaf composed of a central leaf stalk with two or more leaflets. A compound leaf has a bud at its base; a leaflet does not. (*Compare:* Simple leaf)

Cone: A fruit consisting of scales arranged in an overlapping or spiral fashion around a central core; seeds develop between the scales. (*Compare:* Berry, Capsule, Drupe, Pepo, Pome, Pseudocarp)

Coniferous: A tree with needle-like or scale-like leaves (usually evergreen), whose seeds are contained in cones. (*Compare:* Hardwood)

Corymb: A flat-topped, umbrella-like cluster of multiple fruits, each growing on a stemlet that is attached to a single point on the central fruiting stalk; stemlets are varying in length so all fruits are on the same level. (*Compare:* Umbel)

Crown: A remnant of the flower, found on the base of some fruits; it looks like a circle of pointed, dried leaf tips. Also used to refer to the top of a tree or shrub, particularly one with a rounded appearance.

Dappled: A forested area that receives sunlight broken up by light leaf cover.

Deciduous: A tree or shrub whose leaves fall off at the end of the growing season. (*Compare:* Evergreen)

Dehiscent: A fruit that dries out and splits open to release its seeds; legumes are dehiscent. (*Compare:* Indehiscent)

Doubly compound leaf: A compound leaf consisting of two or more compound blades, attached to the central leaf stalk. Only the main leaf stalk has a bud at the base; the secondary compound leaves are not true leaves, and have no bud.

Doubly toothed leaf: Each leaf tooth has one or more smaller teeth, making for a very jagged edge that alternates between coarse and fine teeth.

Downy: Having fine, soft hairs.

Drupe: A simple, fleshy fruit with a hard pit (stone); the pit typically contains one seed, but can contain more. (*Compare:* Berry, Capsule, Compound drupe, Cone, Pepo, Pome, Pseudocarp)

Elliptic: A leaf that is roughly oval in shape; ends may be pointed or rounded.

Endangered: A native plant whose populations have been depleted by animal predation or over-harvesting, or whose growing area has been reduced by pollution, habitat loss or over-competition from other plants.

Evergreen: Leaves that typically remain green; typically needle-like. (*Compare:* Deciduous)

Filament: A long stalk that holds the anther, the pollen-producing part of a plant.

Flower stalk: A separate stem that carries the flowers but no leaves. Synonymous with fruiting stalk.

Follicle: A dry fruit derived from a single carpel; follicles dry out and split open on one side only to release their seeds. (*Compare:* Legume, Nut)

Fruit: The ripened part of a plant that disperses seeds. (*See* Berry, Capsule, Cone, Drupe, Pepo, Pome, Pseudocarp)

Fruiting stalk: A separate stem that carries the fruits but no leaves. Synonymous with flowering stalk.

Gall: A swelling in the stem of a plant, caused by an insect that has burrowed into the stem.

Gland: A cell, small organ or structure that secretes (discharges) minute amounts of fluids or other substances.

Hardwood: A broad-leaved tree whose seeds are contained in fruits or nuts. (*Compare:* Coniferous)

Indehiscent: A fruit that dries out but does not split open; nuts are indehiscent. (*Compare:* Dehiscent)

Introduced: A plant, often from Europe or Asia, that did not grow naturally in the wild in our area but was planted as an ornamental or a food crop; sometimes planted to control erosion or provide shade. Synonymous with non-native.

Invasive: A plant, generally non-native (introduced), that spreads rapidly and crowds out native plants, shades understory plants, changes soil chemistry or depletes soil of moisture.

Lance-shaped: A leaf that is long and slender, with sides that are almost parallel for much of the length.

Leaf axil: The point at which a leaf stalk (from a simple or compound leaf) joins the stem.

Leaflet: An individual leaf-like member of a compound leaf. A leaflet does not have a bud at its base; only true leaves such as the compound leaf and the simple leaf have a bud at the base.

Legume: A pod containing pea-like seeds; legumes dry out and split open to release their seeds. (*Compare:* Follicle, Nut)

Lenticel: A breathing pore, appearing as a bump or raised line in the bark of a tree or woody shrub.

Lobed leaf: A leaf that has several distinct sections, typically scalloped or pointed.

Midrib: The central rib of a leaf.

Mixed forest: A forest having both hardwood and coniferous trees.

Multiple fruit: A single fruit formed from multiple flowers that grow together in a cluster.

Node: A joining point between a leaf stem and the main stem or between two stems.

Non-native: A plant, often from Europe or Asia, that did not grow naturally in the wild in our area but was planted as an ornamental or a food crop; sometimes planted to control erosion or provide shade. Synonymous with introduced.

Nut: A large, dry fruit with a hard seedcoat, usually containing a single seed; nuts are indehiscent. (*Compare:* Follicle, Legume)

Opposite attachment: An arrangement of leaves in which individual leaves are attached to the stem directly across from one another. (*Compare:* Alternate attachment, Whorled attachment)

Ovary: A case containing carpels, which hold the ovules (eggs); a component of the pistil.

Paddle-shaped: A leaf that is narrow at the base, widening at or above the midpoint to a broad tip that is typically rounded.

Palmately compound: An arrangement of leaflets in a compound leaf, in which individual leaflets radiate from a central point, similar to fingers radiating from the palm of a hand. (*Compare:* Pinnately compound)

Pectin: A natural thickening agent found in apples and some other fruits; pectin helps jelly and jam "set" or thicken naturally.

Peltate: A leaf whose stem is attached on the underside, slightly away from the base of the leaf. (*Compare:* Clasping, Perfoliate, Sessile)

Pepo: A simple fruit with a tough rind developed from the receptacle. (*Compare:* Berry, Capsule, Cone, Drupe, Pome, Pseudocarp)

Perennial: A plant whose greenery, flowers and fruit die back each season, but which grows again the following year from the same root. (*Compare:* Annual)

Perfoliate: A leaf whose base extends slightly beyond the stem, giving the impression that the stem is growing up through the leaf. (*Compare:* Clasping, Peltate, Sessile)

Petiole: The stemlet that attaches a leaf, or a leaflet, to the stem or leaf stalk.

Photosynthesis: The process by which a plant converts sunlight to food.

Pinnately compound: An arrangement of leaflets in a compound leaf, in which individual leaflets are arranged either alternately or oppositely along the central leaf stalk. (*Compare:* Palmately compound)

Pistil: The female part of a flower, consisting of an ovary, style and stigma; usually in the center of the flower.

Pome: A simple fruit whose flesh is developed from the receptacle. (*Compare:* Berry, Capsule, Cone, Drupe, Pepo, Pseudocarp)

Pseudocarp: A simple fruit, such as a pome or pepo, whose flesh is developed from a part other than the ovary. (*Compare:* Berry, Capsule, Cone, Drupe, Pepo, Pome)

Raceme: A long cluster of multiple fruits, each growing on a stemlet that is attached to a central fruiting stalk; stemlets are equal in length. (*Compare:* Umbrella-like cluster)

Receptacle: An enlarged area at the base of a flower, just below the reproductive structures. In compound drupes, the receptacle is the core of the fruit.

Rhizome: An underground stem that produces lateral shoots and roots at intervals.

Runner: A shoot growing from the base of a shrub, capable of rooting along its length.

Sepal: A type of petal in the outermost group at the base of a flower; typically green and leaf-like. Sepals often enclose and protect the flower when in bud.

Serrated: Finely toothed.

Sessile: A leaf that attaches directly to the stem, with no leaf stalk. (*Compare:* Clasping, Peltate, Perfoliate)

Simple leaf: A single, true leaf with a bud at the base of the leaf stem. (*Compare:* Compound leaf, Leaflet)

Sinus: The depression between lobes of a leaf.

Spadix: A club-like structure with many small flowers (later, fruits) clustered tightly together on a spike; usually partially enclosed by a spathe.

Spathe: A large petal-like structure, sometimes curled into a tube-like shape, that partially surrounds a flowering cluster called a spadix.

Stamen: The male part of a flower, consisting of the anther and filament; usually around the edges of the inside of a flower.

Stemlet: A secondary stem that connects a fruit or a leaf to the main stem.

Stigma: The part of a flower that collects and germinates pollen, which it then sends down the style into the ovules contained in the ovary.

Style: A long stalk that holds the stigma, which is the pollen-gathering part of a plant.

Subshrub: A perennial with a woody base and non-woody stems.

Sucker: A shoot that grows from the underground roots at the base of a plant; suckering plants often form thickets.

Tendril: A thread-like appendage, found on climbing vines, that coils around other plants or objects.

Terminal leaflet: The leaflet at the end of a compound leaf that has an uneven numbers of leaflets; other leaflets are paired.

Thicket: A dense cluster of shrubs, trees or brushy plants.

Toothed leaf: A leaf with multiple points (teeth) around the edge. Teeth can be sharply pointed or rounded. *See also* Doubly toothed leaf.

Trifoliate: A compound leaf with three leaflets.

True leaf: A simple leaf, or a compound leaf, with a bud at the base. (*Compare:* Leaflet)

Tuber: A thickened portion of an underground stem, containing buds from which new growth will sprout; the common potato is a well-known tuber.

Umbel: A rounded, umbrella-like cluster of multiple fruits, each growing on a stemlet that is attached to a single point on the central fruiting stalk; stemlets are equal in length. (*Compare:* Corymb)

Umbrella-like cluster: A cluster of multiple fruits, each growing on a stemlet that is attached to a single point on the central fruiting stalk. If stemlets are equal in length, the cluster is rounded (umbel); if stalks are varying in length, the cluster has a flat top (corymb). (*Compare:* Raceme)

Whorled attachment: An arrangement of leaves in which three or more leaves attach to a central point. (*Compare:* Alternate attachment, Opposite attachment)

INDEX

331

ABOUT THE AUTHOR

Teresa Marrone has been gathering and preparing wild edibles for more than 20 years. She was formerly Managing Editor of a series of outdoors-themed books, and is the author of *Abundantly Wild: Collecting and Cooking Wild Edibles in the Upper Midwest*, as well as numerous other outdoors-related cookbooks. Teresa also writes magazine articles on wild foods and cooking, and has taken up photography in recent years.

Wild Berries & Fruits Field Guide of Illinois, Iowa and Missouri combines her various skills and interests into a clear, concise, easy-to-use book that helps the user appreciate the diversity of the various wild berries and fruits that grow in this region. Teresa lives in Minneapolis with husband Bruce and their Senegal parrot, Tuca.